LENTEN GOSPEL REFLECTIONS

BISHOP ROBERT BARRON

WITH REFLECTION QUESTIONS BY
PEGGY PANDALEON

Published by Word on Fire, Elk Grove Village, IL 60007

Printed in the United States of America

Cover design by Cassie Bielak, typesetting by Marlene Burrell, and interior art direction by Cassie Bielak and Katherine Spitler

ISBN: 978-1-68578-145-3

Library of Congress Control Number: 2024942625

INTRODUCTION

Friends,

Welcome as we journey together toward the great feast of Easter!

For many people, the big feast of the year is Christmas, but for Christians, the truly great feast is Easter. Without Easter, without the Resurrection, we would not have the gift of salvation. Jesus had to rise from the dead, or else he would have just been another failed Messiah and his birth would be a forgotten footnote of history.

That's why Lent is such an important time of year for us. It is the period during which we refocus on the Passion and death of Jesus so that we will be ready to embrace the good news of the Resurrection at Easter.

So, as we begin with Ash Wednesday and its reminder of repentance, let us resolve to do our best each day, knowing that it is not the destination but the journey that will ultimately transform us.

God bless you,

+Robert Barron

Bishop Robert Barron

LENTEN *GOSPEL* REFLECTIONS

MARCH 5, 2025

Ash Wednesday

Matthew 6:1–6, 16–18

Jesus said to his disciples: "Take care not to perform righteous deeds in order that people may see them; otherwise, you will have no recompense from your heavenly Father. When you give alms, do not blow a trumpet before you, as the hypocrites do in the synagogues and in the streets to win the praise of others. Amen, I say to you, they have received their reward. But when you give alms, do not let your left hand know what your right is doing, so that your almsgiving may be secret. And your Father who sees in secret will repay you.

"When you pray, do not be like the hypocrites, who love to stand and pray in the synagogues and on street corners so that others may see them. Amen, I say to you, they have received their reward. But when you pray, go to your inner room, close the door, and pray to your Father in secret. And your Father who sees in secret will repay you.

"When you fast, do not look gloomy like the hypocrites. They neglect their appearance, so that they may appear to others to be fasting. Amen, I say to you, they have received their reward. But when you fast, anoint your head and wash your face, so that you may not appear to be fasting, except to your Father who is hidden. And your Father who sees what is hidden will repay you."

Friends, today's Gospel asks us to do three things: pray, fast, and give alms. Let's focus today on prayer. Studies show that prayer is a very common, very popular activity. Even those who profess no belief in God pray!

What is prayer, and how should we pray? Prayer is intimate communion and conversation with God. Judging from Jesus' own life, prayer is something that we ought to do often, especially at key moments of our lives.

Well, how should we pray? What does it look like? You have to pray with faith, and according to Jesus' model, you have to pray with forgiveness. The efficacy of prayer seems to depend on the reconciliation of differences.

You also have to pray with persistence. One reason that we don't receive what we want through prayer is that we give up too easily. Augustine said that God sometimes delays in giving us what we want because he wants our hearts to expand.

Finally, we have to pray in Jesus' name. In doing so, we are relying on his influence with the Father, trusting that the Father will listen to him.

Reflect: What can you do this Lent to strengthen your prayer life?

MARCH 6, 2025

Thursday after Ash Wednesday

Luke 9:22–25

Jesus said to his disciples: "The Son of Man must suffer greatly and be rejected by the elders, the chief priests, and the scribes, and be killed and on the third day be raised."

Then he said to all, "If anyone wishes to come after me, he must deny himself and take up his cross daily and follow me. For whoever wishes to save his life will lose it, but whoever loses his life for my sake will save it. What profit is there for one to gain the whole world yet lose or forfeit himself?"

Friends, in today's Gospel, the Lord lays out the conditions for discipleship. He makes this demand: "For whoever wishes to save his life will lose it, but whoever loses his life for my sake will save it."

Notice please that this is not simply a question of accepting suffering that happens to befall one. This is not simply a Stoic resignation.

Jesus is telling us actively to take up our crosses, to seek them out, to carry them as he willingly carried his. What Jesus did on the cross was to bear the burden of the world's sin. He bore others' burdens in love. And this is what we must do: proactively seek out ways to lighten other people's loads.

Dietrich Bonhoeffer commented that when the Lord summons a person to discipleship, he calls to him to come and die. When the blind Bartimaeus received his sight, at the midpoint of the Gospel of Mark, he followed Jesus up the road that would lead to Calvary. The way of the Christian life begins and ends with the man who is God dying on a cross.

Reflect: Are you drinking your cup of suffering alongside Jesus? How do you think and feel about that suffering?

MARCH 7, 2025

Friday after Ash Wednesday

Matthew 9:14–15

The disciples of John approached Jesus and said, "Why do we and the Pharisees fast much, but your disciples do not fast?" Jesus answered them, "Can the wedding guests mourn as long as the bridegroom is with them? The days will come when the bridegroom is taken away from them, and then they will fast."

Friends, in today's Gospel, people ask Jesus why his disciples do not fast. He says that as wedding guests, they will not fast while he, the Bridegroom, is with them. But "the days will come," he says, "when the bridegroom is taken away from them, and then they will fast."

Why do we fast? Because we have a hunger for God, which is the deepest hunger. We're meant to get access to that hunger. We're meant to feel it so that it can direct us toward God. Every spiritual master recognizes the danger that if we allow the superficial hunger of our lives to dominate, we never reach the deepest hunger.

Thomas Merton once observed that our desires for food and drink are something like little children in their persistence and tendency to dominate. Unless and until they are disciplined, they will skew the functions of the soul according to their purposes.

And fasting is a way of disciplining the hunger for food and drink. It is a way of quieting those desires by not responding to them immediately, so that the deepest desires emerge. Unless you fast, you might never realize how hungry you are for God.

Reflect: Why do we fast during Lent? How does this practice affect you?

MARCH 8, 2025

Saturday after Ash Wednesday

Luke 5:27–32

Jesus saw a tax collector named Levi sitting at the customs post. He said to him, "Follow me." And leaving everything behind, he got up and followed him. Then Levi gave a great banquet for him in his house, and a large crowd of tax collectors and others were at table with them. The Pharisees and their scribes complained to his disciples, saying, "Why do you eat and drink with tax collectors and sinners?" Jesus said to them in reply, "Those who are healthy do not need a physician, but the sick do. I have not come to call the righteous to repentance but sinners."

Friends, in today's Gospel, Jesus tells Matthew, "Follow me." The call of Jesus addresses the mind, but it is meant to move through the mind into the body, and through the body into the whole of one's life, into the most practical of moves and decisions. "Follow me" has the sense of "apprentice to me" or "walk as I walk; think as I think; choose as I choose." Discipleship entails an entire reworking of the self according to the pattern and manner of Jesus.

Upon hearing the address of the Lord, the tax collector, we are told, "got up and followed him." The Greek word behind "got up" is *anastas*, the same word used to describe the resurrection (*anastasis*) of Jesus from the dead. Following Jesus is indeed a kind of resurrection from the dead, since it involves the transition from a lower form of life to a higher, from a preoccupation with the temporary goods of this world to an immersion in the goodness of God.

Those who have undergone a profound conversion tend to speak of their former life as a kind of illusion, something not entirely real. Thus Paul can say, "I live, no longer I, but Christ lives in me" (Gal. 2:20); Thomas Merton can speak of the "false self" that has given way to the authentic self; and, perhaps most movingly, the father of the prodigal son can say, "This brother of yours was dead and has come to life; he was lost and has been found."

Reflect: Reflect on a time in your life when grace came to you unbidden and without explanation and how you responded.

MARCH 9, 2025

First Sunday of Lent

Luke 4:1–13

Filled with the Holy Spirit, Jesus returned from the Jordan and was led by the Spirit into the desert for forty days, to be tempted by the devil. He ate nothing during those days, and when they were over he was hungry. The devil said to him, "If you are the Son of God, command this stone to become bread." Jesus answered him, "It is written, *One does not live on bread alone.*" Then he took him up and showed him all the kingdoms of the world in a single instant. The devil said to him, "I shall give to you all this power and glory; for it has been handed over to me, and I may give it to whomever I wish. All this will be yours, if you worship me." Jesus said to him in reply, "It is written:

You shall worship the Lord, your God,
and him alone shall you serve."

Then he led him to Jerusalem, made him stand on the parapet of the temple, and said to him, "If you are the Son of God, throw yourself down from here, for it is written:

He will command his angels concerning you,
to guard you,

and:

With their hands they will support you,
lest you dash your foot against a stone."

Jesus said to him in reply, "It also says, *You shall not put the Lord, your God, to the test.*" When the devil had finished every temptation, he departed from him for a time.

Friends, in our Gospel for the First Sunday of Lent, Luke gives us the story of the temptation in the desert. At every point in the Gospels, we are meant to identify with Jesus. God became man that man might become God. We participate in him and thereby learn what a godly life is like.

Jesus has just been baptized; he has just learned his deepest identity and mission. And now he confronts—as we all must—the great temptations. What precisely is entailed in being the beloved Son of God?

First, the tempter urges him to use his divine power to satisfy his bodily desires, which Jesus dismisses with a word. Having failed at his first attempt, the devil shifts to perhaps the greatest of the temptations: power. Power is extremely seductive. Many would gladly eschew material things or attention or fame in order to get it. Jesus' great answer in Matthew's account of this story is "Away with you, Satan!" To seek power is to serve Satan—it is stated that bluntly.

Finally, the devil plays a subtler game—he tempts Jesus to manipulate his Father, encouraging him to jump from the temple and let angels save him. It is the temptation faced by Adam and Eve in the garden: deciding how and when God will act.

Reflect: What is the difference between seeking power and having power? When you have power, how should you use it so that you do not serve Satan?

MARCH 10, 2025

Monday of the First Week of Lent

Matthew 25:31–46

Jesus said to his disciples: "When the Son of Man comes in his glory, and all the angels with him, he will sit upon his glorious throne, and all the nations will be assembled before him. And he will separate them one from another, as a shepherd separates the sheep from the goats. He will place the sheep on his right and the goats on his left. Then the king will say to those on his right, 'Come, you who are blessed by my Father. Inherit the kingdom prepared for you from the foundation of the world. For I was hungry and you gave me food, I was thirsty and you gave me drink, a stranger and you welcomed me, naked and you clothed me, ill and you cared for me, in prison and you visited me.' Then the righteous will answer him and say, 'Lord, when did we see you hungry and feed you, or thirsty and give you drink? When did we see you a stranger and welcome you, or naked and clothe you? When did we see you ill or in prison, and visit you?' And the king will say to them in reply, 'Amen, I say to you, whatever you did for one of these least brothers of mine, you did for me.' Then he will say to those on his left, 'Depart from me, you accursed, into the eternal fire prepared for the Devil and his angels. For I was hungry and you gave me no food, I was thirsty and you gave me no drink, a stranger and you gave me no welcome, naked and you gave me no clothing, ill and in prison, and you did not care for me.' Then they will answer and say, 'Lord, when did we see you hungry or thirsty or a stranger or naked or ill or in prison, and not minister to your needs?' He will answer them, 'Amen, I say to you, what you did not do for one of these least ones, you did not do for me.' And these will go off to eternal punishment, but the righteous to eternal life."

Friends, today's Gospel tells of Christ the King administering the final judgment. To those on his right he will say, "Amen, I say to you, whatever you did for one of the least brothers of mine, you did for me." And to those on his left, "Amen, I say to you, what you did not do for one of these least ones, you did not do for me."

Much of Mother Teresa's day was taken up with prayer, meditation, Mass, Eucharistic Adoration, and the Rosary, but the rest of her time, as we well know, was spent in the grittiest work among the poorest of the poor, practicing the corporal and spiritual works of mercy.

Fr. Paul Murray, the Irish Dominican spiritual writer and sometime advisor to Mother Teresa, relates the following story. He was one day in deep conversation with Mother, searching out the sources of her spirituality and mission. At the end of their long talk, she asked him to spread his hand out on the table and, touching his fingers one by one as she spoke, she said, "You did it to me."

Reflect: How are good works an integral part of believing in Jesus Christ?

MARCH 11, 2025

Tuesday of the First Week of Lent

Matthew 6:7–15

Jesus said to his disciples: "In praying, do not babble like the pagans, who think that they will be heard because of their many words. Do not be like them. Your Father knows what you need before you ask him.

"This is how you are to pray:

Our Father who art in heaven,
    hallowed be thy name,
    thy Kingdom come,
thy will be done,
    on earth as it is in heaven.
Give us this day our daily bread;
and forgive us our trespasses,
    as we forgive those who trespass against us;
and lead us not into temptation,
    but deliver us from evil.

"If you forgive men their transgressions, your heavenly Father will forgive you. But if you do not forgive men, neither will your Father forgive your transgressions."

Friends, today's Gospel gives us the Our Father. It asks that God's will be done "on earth as it is in heaven," but biblical cosmology sees these two realms as interpenetrating fields of force. Heaven, the arena of God and the angels, touches upon and calls out to earth, the arena of humans, animals, plants, and planets.

Salvation, therefore, is a matter of the meeting of heaven and earth, so that God might reign as thoroughly here below as he does on high. Jesus' great prayer, which is constantly on the lips of Christians, is distinctively Jewish in inspiration: "Thy Kingdom come, thy will be done, on earth as it is in heaven."

This is decidedly not a prayer that we might escape from the earth, but rather that earth and heaven might come together. The Lord's Prayer raises to a new level what the prophet Isaiah anticipated: "The earth shall be filled with knowledge of the Lord, as water covers the sea" (Isa. 11:9).

The first Christians saw the Resurrection of Jesus as the commencement of the process by which earth and heaven were being reconciled. They appreciated the risen Christ as the one who would bring the justice of heaven to this world.

Reflect: How is "thy will be done" a critical part of the Lord's Prayer?

MARCH 12, 2025

Wednesday of the First Week of Lent

Luke 11:29–32

While still more people gathered in the crowd, Jesus said to them, "This generation is an evil generation; it seeks a sign, but no sign will be given it, except the sign of Jonah. Just as Jonah became a sign to the Ninevites, so will the Son of Man be to this generation. At the judgment the queen of the south will rise with the men of this generation and she will condemn them, because she came from the ends of the earth to hear the wisdom of Solomon, and there is something greater than Solomon here. At the judgment the men of Nineveh will arise with this generation and condemn it, because at the preaching of Jonah they repented, and there is something greater than Jonah here."

Friends, today in our Gospel, some Pharisees ask Jesus for a sign. And Jesus replies, "No sign will be given it, except the sign of Jonah," who was in the belly of the whale for three days and three nights, foreshadowing Jesus' death and Resurrection.

Jonah was called by God to preach conversion to Nineveh, which is described as an enormously large city. It took, they said, three days to walk through it. I can't help but think of Nineveh as one of our large, modern cities, a center of all sorts of worldly activity and preoccupation.

What would its conversion look like? A turning back to God as the only enduring good. After hearing the word of Jonah, the Ninevites "proclaimed a fast and all of them, great and small, put on sackcloth" (Jon. 3:5). What is the purpose of these ascetic practices? To wean people away from an attachment to worldly pleasures.

Go beyond the mind that you have. Repent. Live as though nothing in this world finally matters. And you will be living in the kingdom of God!

Reflect: How is fasting tied to repentance? What is a contemporary version of putting on sackcloth and ashes?

MARCH 13, 2025

Thursday of the First Week of Lent

Matthew 7:7–12

Jesus said to his disciples: "Ask and it will be given to you; seek and you will find; knock and the door will be opened to you. For everyone who asks, receives; and the one who seeks, finds; and to the one who knocks, the door will be opened. Which one of you would hand his son a stone when he asked for a loaf of bread, or a snake when he asked for a fish? If you then, who are wicked, know how to give good gifts to your children, how much more will your heavenly Father give good things to those who ask him.

"Do to others whatever you would have them do to you. This is the law and the prophets."

Friends, today's Gospel assures us of the power of prayer. When some people ask in a spirit of trust, really believing that what they are asking for will happen, it happens. Just as Jesus suggests in the Gospel, "Everyone who asks, receives; and the one who seeks, finds; and to the one who knocks, the door will be opened."

The power of prayer is the confidence that we are being guided and cared for, even when that guidance and care are not immediately apparent. It is what allows someone to live in detachment from all the ups and downs of life. In the language of St. Ignatius of Loyola, "We should not prefer health to sickness, riches to poverty, honor to dishonor, a long life to a short life. . . . Our one desire and choice should be what is more conducive to the end for which we are created . . . to praise, reverence, and serve God our Lord."

Those who live in that kind of detachment are free, and because they are free, they are powerful. They are beyond the threats that arise in the context of this world. This is the source of *dynamis*, real power. This is the power that Martin Luther King Jr., Dorothy Day, and John Paul II wielded: world-changing power.

Reflect: How can prayer be both active ("ask, seek, knock") and also detached? What is the source of this detachment?

MARCH 14, 2025

Friday of the First Week of Lent

Matthew 5:20–26

Jesus said to his disciples: "I tell you, unless your righteousness surpasses that of the scribes and Pharisees, you will not enter into the Kingdom of heaven.

"You have heard that it was said to your ancestors, *You shall not kill; and whoever kills will be liable to judgment.* But I say to you, whoever is angry with his brother will be liable to judgment, and whoever says to his brother, *Raqa*, will be answerable to the Sanhedrin, and whoever says, 'You fool,' will be liable to fiery Gehenna. Therefore, if you bring your gift to the altar, and there recall that your brother has anything against you, leave your gift there at the altar, go first and be reconciled with your brother, and then come and offer your gift. Settle with your opponent quickly while on the way to court. Otherwise your opponent will hand you over to the judge, and the judge will hand you over to the guard, and you will be thrown into prison. Amen, I say to you, you will not be released until you have paid the last penny."

Friends, our Gospel for today is taken from the Sermon on the Mount. Jesus has symbolically established himself as the new Moses, giving a law upon a mountain. His "You have heard that it was said . . . but I say . . ." has revealed that he has authority even over the Torah.

To be clear, the Law is not being abrogated here; it is being intensified. The Law was always meant to bring humanity into line with divinity. In the beginning, this alignment was at a fairly basic level. But now that the definitive Moses has appeared, the alignment is becoming absolute, radical, complete.

And so Jesus teaches, "You have heard that it was said to your ancestors, *You shall not kill; and whoever kills will be liable to judgment.* But I say to you, whoever is angry with his brother will be liable to judgment." Killing is an action, but that action is rooted in a more fundamental dysfunction: a hateful attitude, a disordered soul, a basic misperception of reality. To be utterly like God, we obviously have to eliminate cruel and hateful actions; but we have to go deeper, eliminating cruel and hateful thoughts and attitudes. For God *is* love, right through.

Reflect: Is there a lack of forgiveness in you somewhere?

MARCH 15, 2025

Saturday of the First Week of Lent

Matthew 5:43–48

Jesus said to his disciples: "You have heard that it was said, *You shall love your neighbor and hate your enemy.* But I say to you, love your enemies, and pray for those who persecute you, that you may be children of your heavenly Father, for he makes his sun rise on the bad and the good, and causes rain to fall on the just and the unjust. For if you love those who love you, what recompense will you have? Do not the tax collectors do the same? And if you greet your brothers and sisters only, what is unusual about that? Do not the pagans do the same? So be perfect, just as your heavenly Father is perfect."

Friends, once again our Gospel today is taken from Jesus' Sermon on the Mount. It is one of the most puzzling texts in the New Testament. It speaks of loving our enemies. Not tolerating them or vaguely accepting them but loving them. When you hate your enemy, you confirm him as your enemy. But when you love him in response to his hatred, you confuse and confound him, taking away the very energy that feeds his hatred.

There is a form of oriental martial arts called aikido. The idea of aikido is to absorb the aggressive energy of your opponent, moving with it, continually frustrating him until he comes to the point of realizing that fighting is useless.

Some have pointed out that there is a great deal of this in Jesus' strategy of nonviolence and love of the enemy. You creatively absorb the aggression of your opponent, channeling it back against him, to show him the futility of violence. So when someone insults you, send back a compliment instead of an insult.

Reflect: Have you ever asked God to give you the grace to love "unlovable" people the way he loves them? If so, what happened? If not, why not?

MARCH 16, 2025

Second Sunday of Lent

Luke 9:28b–36

Jesus took Peter, John, and James and went up the mountain to pray. While he was praying his face changed in appearance and his clothing became dazzling white. And behold, two men were conversing with him, Moses and Elijah, who appeared in glory and spoke of his exodus that he was going to accomplish in Jerusalem. Peter and his companions had been overcome by sleep, but becoming fully awake, they saw his glory and the two men standing with him. As they were about to part from him, Peter said to Jesus, "Master, it is good that we are here; let us make three tents, one for you, one for Moses, and one for Elijah." But he did not know what he was saying. While he was still speaking, a cloud came and cast a shadow over them, and they became frightened when they entered the cloud. Then from the cloud came a voice that said, "This is my chosen Son; listen to him." After the voice had spoken, Jesus was found alone. They fell silent and did not at that time tell anyone what they had seen.

Friends, today's Gospel recounts the story of the Transfiguration. Here, the glorified Jesus represents the fulfillment of the Old Testament revelation, symbolized by Moses, representing the Law, and Elijah, representing the prophets.

Let's look at the two basic divisions. God gave the Torah, the Law, to his people, in order that they might become a priestly people, a holy nation, a people set apart, in the hopes that they would then function as a sort of magnet to the rest of the world. But the Law didn't take. From the very beginning, the people turned away from its dictates and became as bad as the nations around them.

And then the prophets. Over and again we hear the call to be faithful to the Torah, to follow the ways of the Lord. The prophets turn on Israel itself repeatedly, reminding her of her sinfulness.

And then came Jesus, God and man. Jesus did what no hero of Judaism had ever done: fulfilled the Law, remained utterly obedient to the demands of the Father, even to the point of laying down his life. He brought the Torah and the prophets thereby to fulfillment.

Reflect: How is it that even though we are sinners, we can also be transfigured and glorified if we live in and through Jesus?

MARCH 17, 2025

Monday of the Second Week of Lent

Luke 6:36–38

Jesus said to his disciples: "Be merciful, just as your Father is merciful.

"Stop judging and you will not be judged. Stop condemning and you will not be condemned. Forgive and you will be forgiven. Give and gifts will be given to you; a good measure, packed together, shaken down, and overflowing, will be poured into your lap. For the measure with which you measure will in return be measured out to you."

Friends, in today's Gospel, Jesus calls us to "be merciful, just as your Father is merciful."

Mercy or tender compassion (*chesed* in the Hebrew of the Old Testament) is God's most distinctive characteristic. St. Augustine reminded us that we are, by our very nature, ordered to God. But since God is tender mercy, "having" God is tantamount to exercising compassion, being merciful ourselves.

And attend to what Jesus says next: "Stop judging and you will not be judged. Stop condemning and you will not be condemned. Forgive and you will be forgiven. Give and gifts will be given to you." According to the "physics" of the spiritual order, the more one draws on the divine life, the more one receives that life, precisely because it is a gift and is properly infinite. God's life is had, as it were, on the fly: when you receive it as a gift, you must give it away, since it only exists in gift form, and then you will find more of it flooding into your heart.

If you want to be happy, Jesus is saying, this divine love, this *chesed* of God, must be central to your life; it must be your beginning, your middle, and your end.

Reflect: How have you "regifted" God's love? When are you tempted to hang on to it and not give it away?

MARCH 18, 2025

Tuesday of the Second Week of Lent

Matthew 23:1–12

Jesus spoke to the crowds and to his disciples, saying, "The scribes and the Pharisees have taken their seat on the chair of Moses. Therefore, do and observe all things whatsoever they tell you, but do not follow their example. For they preach but they do not practice. They tie up heavy burdens hard to carry and lay them on people's shoulders, but they will not lift a finger to move them. All their works are performed to be seen. They widen their phylacteries and lengthen their tassels. They love places of honor at banquets, seats of honor in synagogues, greetings in marketplaces, and the salutation 'Rabbi.' As for you, do not be called 'Rabbi.' You have but one teacher, and you are all brothers. Call no one on earth your father; you have but one Father in heaven. Do not be called 'Master'; you have but one master, the Christ. The greatest among you must be your servant. Whoever exalts himself will be humbled; but whoever humbles himself will be exalted."

Friends, in today's Gospel, Jesus turns his sharp eye and withering critique on the many ways that religious leaders fall into corruption. What precisely is bothering Jesus? Some religious leaders get their kicks from burdening people, laying the law on them heavily, making demands that are terrible, exulting in their own moral superiority.

At the core of Jesus' program is a willingness to bear other people's burdens, to help them carry their loads. And this applies to the moral life as well. If we lay the burden of God's law on people, we must be willing, at the same time, to help them bear it.

Another classic problem with religious people and especially religious leaders: they use the law and morality as a means of inflating the ego. The trouble is that this drug wears off rather quickly, and then they want more of it. They need a greater title, more respect, more recognition.

What is Jesus' recommendation for those caught in this dilemma? To be great is to be a servant: lowly, simple, often forgotten. Eschew marks of respect; don't seek them. Be satisfied with doing your work, whatever it is, on behalf of God's kingdom.

Reflect: Reflect on how pride becomes a burden and how humility frees and elevates.

MARCH 19, 2025

Solemnity of Saint Joseph, Spouse of the Blessed Virgin Mary

Matthew 1:16, 18–21, 24a (or Luke 2:41–51a)

Jacob was the father of Joseph, the husband of Mary. Of her was born Jesus who is called the Christ.

Now this is how the birth of Jesus Christ came about. When his mother Mary was betrothed to Joseph, but before they lived together, she was found with child through the Holy Spirit. Joseph her husband, since he was a righteous man, yet unwilling to expose her to shame, decided to divorce her quietly. Such was his intention when, behold, the angel of the Lord appeared to him in a dream and said, "Joseph, son of David, do not be afraid to take Mary your wife into your home. For it is through the Holy Spirit that this child has been conceived in her. She will bear a son and you are to name him Jesus, because he will save his people from their sins." When Joseph awoke, he did as the angel of the Lord had commanded him and took his wife into his home.

Friends, today's Gospel centers on the intriguing figure of Joseph. Joseph is one of the most beloved of the saints, featured in countless works of art and prominent in the devotional lives of many.

We know almost nothing about him, yet some very powerful spiritual themes emerge in the accounts of Joseph. He had become betrothed to Mary, and this union had been blessed by God. And then he finds that his betrothed is pregnant.

This must have been an emotional maelstrom for him. And, at a deeper level, it is a spiritual crisis. What does God want him to do? Then the angel appears to him in a dream and tells him, "Joseph, son of David, do not be afraid to take Mary your wife into your home." He realizes at that moment that these puzzling events are part of a much greater plan of God's. What appears to be a disaster from his perspective is meaningful from God's perspective.

Joseph was willing to cooperate with the divine plan, though he in no way knew its contours or deepest purpose. Like Mary at the Annunciation, he trusted and let himself be led.

Reflect: Think of the last crisis you encountered. Did you handle it in light of the theo-drama (God's plans and purposes) or in light of an ego-drama (your own plans and purposes)?

MARCH 20, 2025

Thursday of the Second Week of Lent

Luke 16:19–31

Jesus said to the Pharisees: "There was a rich man who dressed in purple garments and fine linen and dined sumptuously each day. And lying at his door was a poor man named Lazarus, covered with sores, who would gladly have eaten his fill of the scraps that fell from the rich man's table. Dogs even used to come and lick his sores. When the poor man died, he was carried away by angels to the bosom of Abraham. The rich man also died and was buried, and from the netherworld, where he was in torment, he raised his eyes and saw Abraham far off and Lazarus at his side. And he cried out, 'Father Abraham, have pity on me. Send Lazarus to dip the tip of his finger in water and cool my tongue, for I am suffering torment in these flames.' Abraham replied, 'My child, remember that you received what was good during your lifetime while Lazarus likewise received what was bad; but now he is comforted here, whereas you are tormented. Moreover, between us and you a great chasm is established to prevent anyone from crossing who might wish to go from our side to yours or from your side to ours.' He said, 'Then I beg you, father, send him to my father's house, for I have five brothers, so that he may warn them, lest they too come to this place of torment.' But Abraham replied, 'They have Moses and the prophets. Let them listen to them.' He said, 'Oh no, father Abraham, but if someone from the dead goes to them, they will repent.' Then Abraham said, 'If they will not listen to Moses and the prophets, neither will they be persuaded if someone should rise from the dead.'"

Friends, today's Gospel focuses on the parable of the rich man and Lazarus. The rich man "dressed in purple garments and fine linen and dined sumptuously each day," while lying at his door was a poor man named Lazarus, "who would gladly have eaten his fill of the scraps that fell from the rich man's table."

God is not pleased with this kind of economic inequality, and he burns with a passion to set things right. This theme came roaring up out of the Bible and into the Christian tradition, and it echoes up and down the centuries. Even though it makes us uncomfortable—and God knows it does, especially those of us who live in the most affluent society in the world—we can't avoid it, because it's everywhere in the Bible.

St. Thomas Aquinas says that we must distinguish between ownership and use of private property. We have a right to ownership through our hard work, through our inheritance. Fair enough. But with regard to the use of those things—how we use them, why we use them—then, says Thomas, we must always be concerned first for the common good and not our own. This especially includes Lazarus at our gate: those who are suffering and most in need.

Reflect: Make a list of how you use your property for the common good. Try to add to that list before Easter.

MARCH 21, 2025

Friday of the Second Week of Lent

Matthew 21:33–43, 45–46

Jesus said to the chief priests and the elders of the people: "Hear another parable. There was a landowner who planted a vineyard, put a hedge around it, dug a wine press in it, and built a tower. Then he leased it to tenants and went on a journey. When vintage time drew near, he sent his servants to the tenants to obtain his produce. But the tenants seized the servants and one they beat, another they killed, and a third they stoned. Again he sent other servants, more numerous than the first ones, but they treated them in the same way. Finally, he sent his son to them, thinking, 'They will respect my son.' But when the tenants saw the son, they said to one another, 'This is the heir. Come, let us kill him and acquire his inheritance.' They seized him, threw him out of the vineyard, and killed him. What will the owner of the vineyard do to those tenants when he comes?" They answered him, "He will put those wretched men to a wretched death and lease his vineyard to other tenants who will give him the produce at the proper times." Jesus said to them,

"Did you never read in the Scriptures:
The stone that the builders rejected
has become the cornerstone;
by the Lord has this been done,
and it is wonderful in our eyes?
Therefore, I say to you, the Kingdom of God will be taken away from you and given to a people that will produce its fruit." When the chief priests and the Pharisees heard his parables, they knew that he was speaking about them. And although they were attempting to arrest him, they feared the crowds, for they regarded him as a prophet.

Friends, just before his Passion and death, Jesus tells this striking story of the landowner who planted a vineyard. The fertile vineyard stands for Israel, his chosen people. But it could be broadened out to include the world. What do we learn from this beautiful image? That God has made for his people a place where they can find rest, enjoyment, and good work.

We—Israel, the Church, the world—are not the owners of this vineyard; we are tenants. One of the most fundamental spiritual mistakes we can make is to think that we own the world. We are tenants, entrusted with the responsibility of caring for it, but everything that we have and are is on loan. Our lives are not about us.

Christ is God's judgment. We are all under his judgment. In the measure that we reject him or refuse to listen to him, we place our tenancy in jeopardy. And so the great question that arises from this reading: How am I using the gifts that God gave me for God's purposes? My money? My time? My talents? My creativity? My relationships? All is for God, and thus all is under God's judgment.

Reflect: In what ways are you sensitive to the responsibility of caring for God's creation?

MARCH 22, 2025

Saturday of the Second Week of Lent

Luke 15:1–3, 11–32

Tax collectors and sinners were all drawing near to listen to Jesus, but the Pharisees and scribes began to complain, saying, "This man welcomes sinners and eats with them." So to them Jesus addressed this parable. "A man had two sons, and the younger son said to his father, 'Father, give me the share of your estate that should come to me.' So the father divided the property between them. After a few days, the younger son collected all his belongings and set off to a distant country where he squandered his inheritance on a life of dissipation. When he had freely spent everything, a severe famine struck that country, and he found himself in dire need. So he hired himself out to one of the local citizens who sent him to his farm to tend the swine. And he longed to eat his fill of the pods on which the swine fed, but nobody gave him any. Coming to his senses he thought, 'How many of my father's hired workers have more than enough food to eat, but here am I, dying from hunger. I shall get up and go to my father and I shall say to him, "Father, I have sinned against heaven and against you. I no longer deserve to be called your son; treat me as you would treat one of your hired workers."' So he got up and went back to his father. While he was still a long way off, his father caught sight of him, and was filled with compassion. He ran to his son, embraced him and kissed him. His son said to him, 'Father, I have sinned against heaven and against you; I no longer deserve to be called your son.' But his father ordered his servants, 'Quickly, bring the finest robe and put it on him; put a ring on his finger and sandals on his feet. Take the fattened calf and slaughter it. Then let us celebrate with a feast, because this son of mine was dead, and has come to life again; he was lost, and has been found.' Then the celebration began. Now the older son had been out in the field and, on his way back, as he neared the house, he heard the sound of music and dancing. He called one of the servants and asked what this might mean. The servant said to him, 'Your brother has returned and your father has slaughtered the fattened calf because he has him back safe and sound.' He became angry, and when he refused to enter the house, his father came out and pleaded with him. He said to his father in reply, 'Look, all these years I served you and not once did I disobey your orders; yet you never gave me even a young goat to feast on with my friends. But when your son returns who swallowed up your property with prostitutes, for him you slaughter the fattened calf.' He said to him, 'My son, you are here with me always; everything I have is yours. But now we must celebrate and rejoice, because your brother was dead and has come to life again; he was lost and has been found.'"

•

Friends, our Gospel today is Jesus' best-known parable, and perhaps the greatest story ever told. It tells us practically everything we need to know about our relationship to God, if we but attend to the details carefully.

The younger son asks for his share of the estate and quickly squanders it in a faraway land—and so it always goes. We are the children of God; we have been given life, being, everything by him; we exist through him at every moment. What is represented here so vividly is the moment of sin, which means rupture or division.

So the son is forced to hire himself out so as to become a feeder of pigs. And no one gives him anything. Coming to his senses at last, he decides to break away and return to his father.

The father sees him from a long way off, and then, throwing respectability to the wind, he comes running out to meet him.

The Bible is not the story of our quest for God, but of God's passionate, relentless quest for us. He puts a ring on his son's finger—the ring of marriage, symbolizing the reestablishment of a right relationship between us and God.

Reflect: Have you ever turned your back on God? How did he pursue you and bring you back to himself?

MARCH 23, 2025

Third Sunday of Lent

Luke 13:1–9

Some people told Jesus about the Galileans whose blood Pilate had mingled with the blood of their sacrifices. Jesus said to them in reply, "Do you think that because these Galileans suffered in this way they were greater sinners than all other Galileans? By no means! But I tell you, if you do not repent, you will all perish as they did! Or those eighteen people who were killed when the tower at Siloam fell on them—do you think they were more guilty than everyone else who lived in Jerusalem? By no means! But I tell you, if you do not repent, you will all perish as they did!"

And he told them this parable: "There once was a person who had a fig tree planted in his orchard, and when he came in search of fruit on it but found none, he said to the gardener, 'For three years now I have come in search of fruit on this fig tree but have found none. So cut it down. Why should it exhaust the soil?' He said to him in reply, 'Sir, leave it for this year also, and I shall cultivate the ground around it and fertilize it; it may bear fruit in the future. If not you can cut it down.'"

Friends, in today's Gospel, Jesus tells the parable of the fig tree that the owner cursed because it bore no fruit. On a deeper level, we may understand it to mean that the Lord expects us to bear spiritual fruit.

The fruit of the Spirit is the universal, all-embracing consequence of the Spirit's presence in us. All people who live in the Spirit should manifest these qualities. The word "fruit" is especially good in this context.

In Psalm 1 we find this comparison: "They are like trees planted by streams of water, which yield their fruit in its season, and their leaves do not wither." The Spirit is this stream; when we are planted near it, we blossom.

Well, what are these fruits of the Holy Spirit? In the fifth chapter of Galatians, Paul enumerates them: "love, joy, peace, patience, kindness, generosity, faithfulness, gentleness, self-control" (Gal. 5:22). When discerning whether the Spirit is living in you, in determining whether you are walking the right path, these are wonderful criteria.

Reflect: What does the lesson of the barren fig tree teach us about what is important in God's mind?

MARCH 24, 2025

Monday of the Third Week of Lent

Luke 4:24–30

Jesus said to the people in the synagogue at Nazareth: "Amen, I say to you, no prophet is accepted in his own native place. Indeed, I tell you, there were many widows in Israel in the days of Elijah when the sky was closed for three and a half years and a severe famine spread over the entire land. It was to none of these that Elijah was sent, but only to a widow in Zarephath in the land of Sidon. Again, there were many lepers in Israel during the time of Elisha the prophet; yet not one of them was cleansed, but only Naaman the Syrian." When the people in the synagogue heard this, they were all filled with fury. They rose up, drove him out of the town, and led him to the brow of the hill on which their town had been built, to hurl him down headlong. But he passed through the midst of them and went away.

Friends, in today's Gospel, Jesus' hometown rejects him as a prophet. And I want to say a word about your role as a prophet.

When most laypeople hear about prophecy, they sit back and their eyes glaze over. "That's something for the priests and the bishops to worry about; they're the modern-day prophets. I don't have that call or that responsibility."

Well, think again! Vatican II emphasized the universal call to holiness, rooted in the dynamics of Baptism. Every baptized person is conformed unto Christ—priest, prophet, and king. Whenever you assist at Mass, you are exercising your priestly office, participating in the worship of God. Whenever you direct your kids to discover their mission in the Church, or provide guidance to someone in the spiritual life, you are exercising your kingly office.

As a baptized individual, you are commissioned as a prophet—which is to say, a speaker of God's truth. And the prophetic word is not your own. It is not the result of your own meditations on the spiritual life, as valuable and correct as those may be. The prophetic word is the word of God given to you by God.

Reflect: How would you evaluate your role as prophet—that is, a speaker of God's truth?

MARCH 25, 2025

Solemnity of the Annunciation of the Lord

Luke 1:26–38

The angel Gabriel was sent from God to a town of Galilee called Nazareth, to a virgin betrothed to a man named Joseph, of the house of David, and the virgin's name was Mary. And coming to her, he said, "Hail, full of grace! The Lord is with you." But she was greatly troubled at what was said and pondered what sort of greeting this might be. Then the angel said to her, "Do not be afraid, Mary, for you have found favor with God. Behold, you will conceive in your womb and bear a son, and you shall name him Jesus. He will be great and will be called Son of the Most High, and the Lord God will give him the throne of David his father, and he will rule over the house of Jacob forever, and of his Kingdom there will be no end." But Mary said to the angel, "How can this be, since I have no relations with a man?" And the angel said to her in reply, "The Holy Spirit will come upon you, and the power of the Most High will overshadow you. Therefore the child to be born will be called holy, the Son of God. And behold, Elizabeth, your relative, has also conceived a son in her old age, and this is the sixth month for her who was called barren; for nothing will be impossible for God." Mary said, "Behold, I am the handmaid of the Lord. May it be done to me according to your word." Then the angel departed from her.

Friends, in today's Gospel, the angel Gabriel appears to Mary and announces that she will conceive the Messiah. Mary, understandably surprised, asks, "How can this be, since I have no relations with a man?" to which the angel replies, "The Holy Spirit will come upon you, and the power of the Most High will overshadow you."

The virginity of the mother of Christ is fitting for a number of reasons. First, it indicates, as clearly as possible, that God is involved in the coming to be of Jesus. Though human cooperation, at both the physical and moral level, is required, the Incarnation would not have happened without a gracious divine initiative.

Further, it signals that the Incarnation involves not simply a revolution in the moral and spiritual order but an entirely new creation. Just as Adam, on the biblical telling, is made through the direct causality of God, so the New Adam is made *de novo*, and not in the ordinary course.

Finally, the virginity of Mary is a sign of the purity and completeness of her devotion to God, making her a fit vessel for the divine Messiah. She becomes mother in the physical order, though she is given utterly over to God; she is, as classical Christian piety would have it, spouse of the Holy Spirit. All of this, one might argue, is summed up in the greeting that the angel gives Mary at the Annunciation, the most sublime offered to any human being in the biblical tradition: *kecharitomene*, "full of grace."

Reflect: Who is Mary to you personally? What is her place in your life?

MARCH 26, 2025

Wednesday of the Third Week of Lent

Matthew 5:17–19

Jesus said to his disciples: "Do not think that I have come to abolish the law or the prophets. I have come not to abolish but to fulfill. Amen, I say to you, until heaven and earth pass away, not the smallest letter or the smallest part of a letter will pass from the law, until all things have taken place. Therefore, whoever breaks one of the least of these commandments and teaches others to do so will be called least in the Kingdom of heaven. But whoever obeys and teaches these commandments will be called greatest in the Kingdom of heaven."

Friends, in today's Gospel, Jesus promises that he has not come to abolish the Law, but to fulfill it. Matthew says that Jesus went up a mountain, sat down, and commenced to teach, calling to mind Moses, who went up Mount Sinai to receive the Ten Commandments from God.

Therefore, Jesus is being presented here as the New Moses who will promulgate from this Galilean mountain the definitive Law. I realize that this immediately poses a problem for contemporary readers, who are put off by a religion that leads with laws, rules, and prohibitions. An Irish wag once summed up the Catholicism that he was taught with this phrase: "In the beginning was the word, and the word was no!"

Since the Ten Commandments have been honored mostly in the breach, why should anyone think it a good idea to introduce new and even more stringent laws? But then we attend to the first word out of the mouth of the lawgiver: "Blessed," "Happy." The law that the New Moses offers is a pattern of life that promises to make us happy.

Reflect: What are your hopes, dreams, and longings? How does Jesus fulfill them?

MARCH 27, 2025

Thursday of the Third Week of Lent

Luke 11:14–23

Jesus was driving out a demon that was mute, and when the demon had gone out, the mute man spoke and the crowds were amazed. Some of them said, "By the power of Beelzebul, the prince of demons, he drives out demons." Others, to test him, asked him for a sign from heaven. But he knew their thoughts and said to them, "Every kingdom divided against itself will be laid waste and house will fall against house. And if Satan is divided against himself, how will his kingdom stand? For you say that it is by Beelzebul that I drive out demons. If I, then, drive out demons by Beelzebul, by whom do your own people drive them out? Therefore they will be your judges. But if it is by the finger of God that I drive out demons, then the Kingdom of God has come upon you. When a strong man fully armed guards his palace, his possessions are safe. But when one stronger than he attacks and overcomes him, he takes away the armor on which he relied and distributes the spoils. Whoever is not with me is against me, and whoever does not gather with me scatters."

Friends, in today's Gospel, we learn of a person possessed by a demon. Jesus meets the man and drives out the demon, but then is immediately accused of being in league with Satan. Some of the witnesses say, "By the power of Beelzebul, the prince of demons, he drives out demons."

Jesus' response is wonderful in its logic and laconicism: "Every kingdom divided against itself will be laid waste and house will fall against house. And if Satan is divided against himself, how will his kingdom stand?"

The demonic power is always one of scattering. It breaks up communion. But Jesus, as always, is the voice of *communio*, of one bringing things back together.

Think back to Jesus' feeding of the five thousand. Facing a large, hungry crowd, his disciples beg him to "dismiss the crowds so that they can go to the villages and buy food for themselves" (Matt. 14:15). But Jesus answers, "There is no need for them to go away; give them some food yourselves" (Matt. 14:16).

Whatever drives the Church apart is an echo of this "dismiss the crowds" impulse, and a reminder of the demonic tendency to divide. In times of trial and threat, this is a very common instinct. We blame, attack, break up, and disperse. But Jesus is right: "There is no need for them to go away."

Reflect: How can you work for unity among all parts of the Body of Christ?

MARCH 28, 2025

Friday of the Third Week of Lent

Mark 12:28–34

One of the scribes came to Jesus and asked him, "Which is the first of all the commandments?" Jesus replied, "The first is this:

Hear, O Israel!
The Lord our God is Lord alone!
You shall love the Lord your God with all your heart,
with all your soul,
with all your mind,
and with all your strength.

The second is this:

You shall love your neighbor as yourself.

There is no other commandment greater than these." The scribe said to him, "Well said, teacher. You are right in saying,

He is One and there is no other than he.

And *to love him with all your heart,*
with all your understanding,
with all your strength,
and to love your neighbor as yourself

is worth more than all burnt offerings and sacrifices." And when Jesus saw that he answered with understanding, he said to him, "You are not far from the Kingdom of God." And no one dared to ask him any more questions.

Friends, in today's Gospel, Jesus asserts that the whole law depends upon two commandments: loving God with everything you have and loving your neighbor as yourself.

This first commandment echoes the Old Testament *shema* prayer found in Deuteronomy: "Hear, O Israel! The LORD is our God, the LORD alone! Therefore, you shall love the LORD, your God, with your whole heart, and with your whole being, and with your whole strength" (Deut. 6:4–5).

What is interesting here is that Jesus does not feel the slightest compulsion to mitigate the exclusivity of the *shema* when he adds the second commandment. The one who is to love his neighbor is precisely the one who is summoned to love the Lord with all his heart, soul, and mind. Nothing prevents the one who utterly and completely loves God from loving, simultaneously, the good things to which God continually gives rise.

Since God is entirely responsible for the being of whatever he creates, and since the world adds nothing to the divine perfection, in loving God, one is implicitly loving everything that God sustains in existence. This is why the spiritual masters can speak of loving God in the first place and then loving everything else for the sake of God.

Reflect: Is it possible to love God and not love your neighbor? Why not?

MARCH 29, 2025

Saturday of the Third Week of Lent

Luke 18:9–14

Jesus addressed this parable to those who were convinced of their own righteousness and despised everyone else. "Two people went up to the temple area to pray; one was a Pharisee and the other was a tax collector. The Pharisee took up his position and spoke this prayer to himself, 'O God, I thank you that I am not like the rest of humanity—greedy, dishonest, adulterous—or even like this tax collector. I fast twice a week, and I pay tithes on my whole income.' But the tax collector stood off at a distance and would not even raise his eyes to heaven but beat his breast and prayed, 'O God, be merciful to me a sinner.' I tell you, the latter went home justified, not the former; for everyone who exalts himself will be humbled, and the one who humbles himself will be exalted."

Friends, today Jesus tells us of the Pharisee and the tax collector—so, stereotypically righteous and unrighteous people—who both enter the temple to pray. But what a world of difference in their manner of praying!

The entire point of religion is to make us humble before God and to open us to the path of love. Everything else is more or less a footnote. Liturgy, prayer, the precepts of the Church, the Commandments, sacraments, sacramentals—all of it—are finally meant to conform us to the way of love. When they instead turn us away from that path, they have been undermined.

Both St. Paul and the Gospel writers—as well as Jesus himself, of course—are intensely aware of this danger. This is precisely why Paul speaks of the dangers of the Law. He knew that people often use the Law as a weapon of aggression: since I know what is right and wrong in some detail, then I am uniquely positioned to point out your flaws. And when I point out your flaws, I elevate myself. In short, the Law, which is a gift from God, has been co-opted for the purposes of the ego.

Reflect: How does the tenor of your prayers reflect who God is in your life?

MARCH 30, 2025

Fourth Sunday of Lent

Luke 15:1–3, 11–32

Tax collectors and sinners were all drawing near to listen to Jesus, but the Pharisees and scribes began to complain, saying, "This man welcomes sinners and eats with them." So to them Jesus addressed this parable. "A man had two sons, and the younger son said to his father, 'Father, give me the share of your estate that should come to me.' So the father divided the property between them. After a few days, the younger son collected all his belongings and set off to a distant country where he squandered his inheritance on a life of dissipation. When he had freely spent everything, a severe famine struck that country, and he found himself in dire need. So he hired himself out to one of the local citizens who sent him to his farm to tend the swine. And he longed to eat his fill of the pods on which the swine fed, but nobody gave him any. Coming to his senses he thought, 'How many of my father's hired workers have more than enough food to eat, but here am I, dying from hunger. I shall get up and go to my father and I shall say to him,

"Father, I have sinned against heaven and against you. I no longer deserve to be called your son; treat me as you would treat one of your hired workers."' So he got up and went back to his father. While he was still a long way off, his father caught sight of him, and was filled with compassion. He ran to his son, embraced him and kissed him. His son said to him, 'Father, I have sinned against heaven and against you; I no longer deserve to be called your son.' But his father ordered his servants, 'Quickly, bring the finest robe and put it on him; put a ring on his finger and sandals on his feet. Take the fattened calf and slaughter it. Then let us celebrate with a feast, because this son of mine was dead, and has come to life again; he was lost, and has been found.' Then the celebration began. Now the older son had been out in the field and, on his way back, as he neared the house, he heard the sound of music and dancing. He called one of the servants and asked what this might mean. The servant said to him, 'Your brother has returned and your father has slaughtered the fattened calf because he has him back safe and sound.' He became angry, and when he refused to enter the house, his father came out and pleaded with him. He said to his father in reply, 'Look, all these years I served you and not once did

I disobey your orders; yet you never gave me even a young goat to feast on with my friends. But when your son returns who swallowed up your property with prostitutes, for him you slaughter the fattened calf.' He said to him, 'My son, you are here with me always; everything I have is yours. But now we must celebrate and rejoice, because your brother was dead and has come to life again; he was lost and has been found.'"

Friends, at the core of today's Gospel is a portrait of our God, who is prodigal. The father stands for the God whose very nature is to give, the God who simply is love. And the younger son stands for all of us sinners who tend to misunderstand how to access the divine love.

Since God exists only in gift form, his life, even in principle, cannot become a possession. Instead, it is "had" only on the fly, only in the measure that it is given away. When we cling to it, it disappears, according to a kind of spiritual physics.

The Greek that lies behind "distant country" in the parable is *chora makra*; that means, literally, "the great emptiness." Trying to turn the divine gift into the ego's possession necessarily results in nothing, nonbeing, the void.

St. John Paul II formulated the principle here as "the law of the gift"—that your being increases inasmuch as you give it away. If clinging and possessing are the marks of the *chora makra*, then the law of the gift is the defining dynamic of the father's house, where the robe and the ring and the fatted calf are on permanent offer.

Reflect: What gifts do you have that you give away freely? What gifts do you cling to?

MARCH 31, 2025

Monday of the Fourth Week of Lent

John 4:43–54

At that time Jesus left [Samaria] for Galilee. For Jesus himself testified that a prophet has no honor in his native place. When he came into Galilee, the Galileans welcomed him, since they had seen all he had done in Jerusalem at the feast; for they themselves had gone to the feast.

Then he returned to Cana in Galilee, where he had made the water wine. Now there was a royal official whose son was ill in Capernaum. When he heard that Jesus had arrived in Galilee from Judea, he went to him and asked him to come down and heal his son, who was near death. Jesus said to him, "Unless you people see signs and wonders, you will not believe." The royal official said to him, "Sir, come down before my child dies." Jesus said to him, "You may go; your son will live." The man believed what Jesus said to him and left. While the man was on his way back, his slaves met him and told him that his boy would live. He asked them when he began to recover. They told him, "The fever left him yesterday, about one in the afternoon." The father realized that just at that time Jesus had said to him, "Your son will live," and he and his whole household came to believe. Now this was the second sign Jesus did when he came to Galilee from Judea.

Friends, our Gospel today tells of Jesus healing a royal official's son. The official asks him to heal his son, who is near death. Jesus says to him, "Unless you people see signs and wonders, you will not believe." But the royal official persists, and Jesus tells him his son will live. The man believes Jesus, and his son recovers.

Theologian Paul Tillich said that "faith" is the most misunderstood word in the religious vocabulary. And this is a tragedy, for faith stands at the very heart of the program; it is the *sine qua non* of the Christian thing. What is it? The opening line of Hebrews 11 has the right definition: "Faith is the realization of what is hoped for and evidence of things not seen."

Faith is a straining ahead toward those things that are, at best, dimly glimpsed. But notice, please, that it is not a craven, hand-wringing, unsure business. It is confident and full of conviction. Think of the great figures of faith, from Abraham to John Paul II: they are anything but shaky, indefinite, questioning people. Like the royal official, they are clear, focused, assured.

Reflect: Are miracles only found in Scripture, or are you open to asking for them and recognizing them even today?

APRIL 1, 2025

Tuesday of the Fourth Week of Lent

John 5:1–16

There was a feast of the Jews, and Jesus went up to Jerusalem. Now there is in Jerusalem at the Sheep Gate a pool called in Hebrew Bethesda, with five porticoes. In these lay a large number of ill, blind, lame, and crippled. One man was there who had been ill for thirty-eight years. When Jesus saw him lying there and knew that he had been ill for a long time, he said to him, "Do you want to be well?" The sick man answered him, "Sir, I have no one to put me into the pool when the water is stirred up; while I am on my way, someone else gets down there before me." Jesus said to him, "Rise, take up your mat, and walk." Immediately the man became well, took up his mat, and walked.

Now that day was a sabbath. So the Jews said to the man who was cured, "It is the sabbath, and it is not lawful for you to carry your mat." He answered them, "The man who made me well told me, 'Take up your mat and walk.'" They asked him, "Who is the man who told you, 'Take it up and walk'?" The man who was healed did not know who it was, for Jesus had slipped away, since there was a crowd there. After this Jesus found him in the temple area and said to him, "Look, you are well; do not sin any more, so that nothing worse may happen to you." The man went and told the Jews that Jesus was the one who had made him well. Therefore, the Jews began to persecute Jesus because he did this on a sabbath.

Friends, in today's Gospel, Jesus heals a man who was physically ill for thirty-eight years. I want to make an observation about another manifestation of Christ's power: his spiritual healing.

The Gospels are filled with accounts of Jesus' healing encounters with those whose spiritual energies are unable to flow. Much of Jesus' ministry consisted in teaching people how to see (the kingdom of God), how to hear (the voice of the Spirit), how to walk (thereby overcoming the paralysis of the heart), how to be free of themselves so as to discover God. It is interesting that Jesus was referred to in the early Church as the Savior (*soter* in Greek and *salvator* in Latin). Both terms speak of the one who brings healing.

The "soul" is that still point at the heart of every person, that deepest center, that point of encounter with the transcendent yet incarnate mystery of God. When the soul is healthy, it is in a living relationship with God; it is firmly rooted in the soil of meaning and is the deepest center of the person.

Reflect: In what way does your soul need spiritual healing?

APRIL 2, 2025

Wednesday of the Fourth Week of Lent

John 5:17–30

Jesus answered the Jews: "My Father is at work until now, so I am at work." For this reason they tried all the more to kill him, because he not only broke the sabbath but he also called God his own father, making himself equal to God.

Jesus answered and said to them, "Amen, amen, I say to you, the Son cannot do anything on his own, but only what he sees the Father doing; for what he does, the Son will do also. For the Father loves the Son and shows him everything that he himself does, and he will show him greater works than these, so that you may be amazed. For just as the Father raises the dead and gives life, so also does the Son give life to whomever he wishes. Nor does the Father judge anyone, but he has given all judgment to the Son, so that all may honor the Son just as they honor the Father. Whoever does not honor the Son does not honor the Father who sent him. Amen, amen, I say to you, whoever hears my word and believes in the one who sent me has eternal life and will not come to condemnation, but has passed from death to life. Amen, amen, I say to you, the hour is coming and is now here when the dead will hear the voice of the Son of God, and those who hear will live. For just as the Father has life in himself, so also he gave to the Son the possession of life in himself. And he gave him power to exercise judgment, because he is the Son of Man. Do not be amazed at this, because the hour is coming in which all who are in the tombs will hear his voice and will come out, those who have done good deeds to the resurrection of life, but those who have done wicked deeds to the resurrection of condemnation.

"I cannot do anything on my own; I judge as I hear, and my judgment is just, because I do not seek my own will but the will of the one who sent me."

Friends, in today's Gospel, we see Jesus as the judge who shows mercy and love. It is hard to read any two pages of the Bible—Old Testament or New—and not find the language of divine judgment.

Think of judgment as a sort of light, which reveals both the positive and the negative. Beautiful things look even more beautiful when the light shines on them; ugly things look even uglier when they come into the light. When the divine light shines, when judgment takes place, something like real love is unleashed.

Someone might avoid seeing the doctor for years, fearful that he will uncover something diseased or deadly. But how much better it is for you when you do, even when the doctor pronounces a harsh "judgment" on your physical condition!

And this is why judgment is the proper activity of a king. It is not the exercise of arbitrary power, but rather an exercise of real love.

Reflect: What do you do to move out of the convenient darkness and allow the light of Christ to shine on your own attitudes and behaviors?

APRIL 3, 2025

Thursday of the Fourth Week of Lent

John 5:31–47

Jesus said to the Jews: "If I testify on my own behalf, my testimony is not true. But there is another who testifies on my behalf, and I know that the testimony he gives on my behalf is true. You sent emissaries to John, and he testified to the truth. I do not accept human testimony, but I say this so that you may be saved. He was a burning and shining lamp, and for a while you were content to rejoice in his light. But I have testimony greater than John's. The works that the Father gave me to accomplish, these works that I perform testify on my behalf that the Father has sent me. Moreover, the Father who sent me has testified on my behalf. But you have never heard his voice nor seen his form, and you do not have his word remaining in you, because you do not believe in the one whom he has sent. You search the Scriptures, because you think you have eternal life through them; even they testify on my behalf. But you do not want to come to me to have life.

"I do not accept human praise; moreover, I know that you do not have the love of God in you. I came in the name of my Father, but you do not accept me; yet if another comes in his own name, you will accept him. How can you believe, when you accept praise from one another and do not seek the praise that comes from the only God? Do not think that I will accuse you before the Father: the one who will accuse you is Moses, in whom you have placed your hope. For if you had believed Moses, you would have believed me, because he wrote about me. But if you do not believe his writings, how will you believe my words?"

Friends, in today's Gospel, Jesus says that his Father's works testify to his identity. Jesus' words are the Father's words, and his deeds are the Father's deeds. His story is the Father's story.

Nature speaks of God, the philosophers say true things about God, the arts can reflect him, the lives of the saints can indicate him—but Jesus is the icon.

We sense in this passage, if I can put it this way, the humility of the Logos. Neither the words nor the deeds of Jesus are "his own." They are received from the Father. The Trinitarian theological tradition respects this when it speaks of the Son as the interior word of the Father and as having received everything from the Father.

Reflect: Jesus says that his works testify that he was sent from the Father. How do your works testify that you are sent by Jesus on mission?

APRIL 4, 2025

Friday of the Fourth Week of Lent

John 7:1–2, 10, 25–30

Jesus moved about within Galilee; he did not wish to travel in Judea, because the Jews were trying to kill him. But the Jewish feast of Tabernacles was near.

But when his brothers had gone up to the feast, he himself also went up, not openly but as it were in secret.

Some of the inhabitants of Jerusalem said, "Is he not the one they are trying to kill? And look, he is speaking openly and they say nothing to him. Could the authorities have realized that he is the Christ? But we know where he is from. When the Christ comes, no one will know where he is from." So Jesus cried out in the temple area as he was teaching and said, "You know me and also know where I am from. Yet I did not come on my own, but the one who sent me, whom you do not know, is true. I know him, because I am from him, and he sent me." So they tried to arrest him, but no one laid a hand upon him, because his hour had not yet come.

Friends, the Gospel for today centers around a theme that we can never speak of enough: the divinity of Jesus. There has been a disturbing tendency in recent years—you can see it clearly in Eckhart Tolle's bestselling book *The Power of Now*—to turn Jesus into an inspiring spiritual teacher, like the Buddha or the Sufi mystics.

But if that's all he is, the heck with him. The Gospels are never content with such a reductive description. Though they present Jesus quite clearly as a teacher, they know that he is infinitely more than that. They affirm that something else is at stake in him and in our relation to him.

In our Gospel today, Jesus plainly declares his relationship with his Father: "I did not come on my own, but the one who sent me, whom you do not know, is true. I know him, because I am from him, and he sent me."

Reflect: What sets Jesus apart from other inspiring religious teachers? What does belief in this quality compel us to do?

APRIL 5, 2025

Saturday of the Fourth Week of Lent

John 7:40–53

Some in the crowd who heard these words of Jesus said, "This is truly the Prophet." Others said, "This is the Christ." But others said, "The Christ will not come from Galilee, will he? Does not Scripture say that the Christ will be of David's family and come from Bethlehem, the village where David lived?" So a division occurred in the crowd because of him. Some of them even wanted to arrest him, but no one laid hands on him.

So the guards went to the chief priests and Pharisees, who asked them, "Why did you not bring him?" The guards answered, "Never before has anyone spoken like this man." So the Pharisees answered them, "Have you also been deceived? Have any of the authorities or the Pharisees believed in him? But this crowd, which does not know the law, is accursed." Nicodemus, one of their members who had come to him earlier, said to them, "Does our law condemn a man before it first hears him and finds out what he is doing?" They answered and said to him, "You are not from Galilee also, are you? Look and see that no prophet arises from Galilee."

Then each went to his own house.

Friends, we see in today's Gospel how Jesus' preaching caused division. Some hearers believed him, but others wanted to arrest him.

The life, preaching, and mission of Jesus are predicated upon the assumption that all is not well with us, that we stand in need of a renovation of vision, attitude, and behavior. A few decades ago, the book *I'm OK—You're OK* appeared. Its title, and the attitude that it embodies, are inimical to Christianity.

The fact of sin is so often overlooked today. Look, no one has ever savored being accused of sin, but especially in our culture now there is an allergy to admitting personal fault.

A salvation religion makes no sense if all is basically fine with us, if all we need is a little sprucing up around the edges. Christian saints are those who can bear the awful revelation that sin is not simply an abstraction or something that other people wrestle with, but a power that lurks and works in them.

When we lose sight of sin, we lose sight of Christianity, which is a salvation religion.

Reflect: Is all basically fine with you, or do you personally need a Savior?

APRIL 6, 2025

Fifth Sunday of Lent

John 8:1–11

Jesus went to the Mount of Olives. But early in the morning he arrived again in the temple area, and all the people started coming to him, and he sat down and taught them. Then the scribes and the Pharisees brought a woman who had been caught in adultery and made her stand in the middle. They said to him, "Teacher, this woman was caught in the very act of committing adultery. Now in the law, Moses commanded us to stone such women. So what do you say?" They said this to test him, so that they could have some charge to bring against him. Jesus bent down and began to write on the ground with his finger. But when they continued asking him, he straightened up and said to them, "Let the one among you who is without sin be the first to throw a stone at her." Again he bent down and wrote on the ground. And in response, they went away one by one, beginning with the elders. So he was left alone with the woman before him. Then Jesus straightened up and said to her, "Woman, where are they? Has no one condemned you?" She replied, "No one, sir." Then Jesus said, "Neither do I condemn you. Go, and from now on do not sin any more."

Friends, our Gospel today tells about the woman that the scribes and Pharisees caught in adultery. Imagine where they were standing when they caught her in the very act. The voyeurism and perversion of these men! Then they come *en masse*, in the terrible enthusiasm of a mob, and they present the case to Jesus.

Now, what does Jesus do in the face of this violent mob? First, he writes on the ground. The mysterious writing might indicate the listing of the sins of each person in the group. As Jesus said in another Gospel, "Remove the wooden beam from your eye first; then you will see clearly to remove the splinter from your brother's eye" (Matt. 7:5).

And then he says, "Let the one among you who is without sin be the first to throw a stone at her." He forces them to turn their accusing glance inward, where it belongs. Instead of projecting their violence outward on a scapegoat, they should honestly name and confront the dysfunction within themselves.

This story, like all the stories in the Gospels, is a foreshadowing of the great story toward which we are tending. Jesus will be put to death by a mob bent on scapegoating violence.

Reflect: Think about the times when you have been guilty of singling out an individual or some group as a scapegoat.

APRIL 7, 2025

Monday of the Fifth Week of Lent

John 8:12–20

Jesus spoke to them again, saying, "I am the light of the world. Whoever follows me will not walk in darkness, but will have the light of life." So the Pharisees said to him, "You testify on your own behalf, so your testimony cannot be verified." Jesus answered and said to them, "Even if I do testify on my own behalf, my testimony can be verified, because I know where I came from and where I am going. But you do not know where I come from or where I am going. You judge by appearances, but I do not judge anyone. And even if I should judge, my judgment is valid, because I am not alone, but it is I and the Father who sent me. Even in your law it is written that the testimony of two men can be verified. I testify on my behalf and so does the Father who sent me." So they said to him, "Where is your father?" Jesus answered, "You know neither me nor my Father. If you knew me, you would know my Father also." He spoke these words while teaching in the treasury in the temple area. But no one arrested him, because his hour had not yet come.

Friends, in our Gospel today, Jesus announces who he is: "I am the light of the world." In John's Gospel, there is a series of "I am" statements: "I am the bread of life"; "I am the good shepherd"; "I am the way, the truth, and the life." And here Jesus issues another of those powerful claims: "I am the light."

Christianity is, above all, a way of seeing. Everything else in Christian life flows from and circles around the transformation of vision. Christians see differently, and that is why their prayer, their worship, their action, their whole way of being in the world have a distinctive accent and flavor.

And Jesus is the way to see. When we are grafted onto him, when we assume his mind and his attitude, when we live his life, we are able to see the world as it is and not through the distorting lens of our fear and our hatred.

Reflect: How is the Christian way of seeing different from the culture's way of seeing?

APRIL 8, 2025

Tuesday of the Fifth Week of Lent

John 8:21–30

Jesus said to the Pharisees: "I am going away and you will look for me, but you will die in your sin. Where I am going you cannot come." So the Jews said, "He is not going to kill himself, is he, because he said, 'Where I am going you cannot come'?" He said to them, "You belong to what is below, I belong to what is above. You belong to this world, but I do not belong to this world. That is why I told you that you will die in your sins. For if you do not believe that I AM, you will die in your sins." So they said to him, "Who are you?" Jesus said to them, "What I told you from the beginning. I have much to say about you in condemnation. But the one who sent me is true, and what I heard from him I tell the world." They did not realize that he was speaking to them of the Father. So Jesus said to them, "When you lift up the Son of Man, then you will realize that I AM, and that I do nothing on my own, but I say only what the Father taught me. The one who sent me is with me. He has not left me alone, because I always do what is pleasing to him." Because he spoke this way, many came to believe in him.

Friends, in today's Gospel, Jesus predicts his death on the cross.

We are meant to see on that cross not simply a violent display, but rather our own ugliness. What brought Jesus to the cross? Stupidity, anger, mistrust, institutional injustice, betrayal of a friend, denial, unspeakable cruelty, scapegoating, fear, etc. In other words, all of our dysfunction is revealed on that cross.

So far so awful. But we can't stop telling the story at this point. Dante and every other spiritual master knew that the only way up is down. When we live in convenient darkness, unaware of our sins, we will never make spiritual progress. So we need the light, however painful it is. But then we can begin to rise.

On the cross of Jesus, we meet our own sin. But we also meet the divine mercy that has taken that sin upon himself in order to swallow it up. We have found, in that cross, the way up. We want to hold up this thing that was considered too horrible to look at. We want to embrace and kiss the very source of our pain.

Reflect: What does the Crucifixion of Jesus mean to you personally? How does this faith affect the way you live?

APRIL 9, 2025

Wednesday of the Fifth Week of Lent

John 8:31–42

Jesus said to those Jews who believed in him, "If you remain in my word, you will truly be my disciples, and you will know the truth, and the truth will set you free." They answered him, "We are descendants of Abraham and have never been enslaved to anyone. How can you say, 'You will become free'?" Jesus answered them, "Amen, amen, I say to you, everyone who commits sin is a slave of sin. A slave does not remain in a household forever, but a son always remains. So if the Son frees you, then you will truly be free. I know that you are descendants of Abraham. But you are trying to kill me, because my word has no room among you. I tell you what I have seen in the Father's presence; then do what you have heard from the Father."

They answered and said to him, "Our father is Abraham." Jesus said to them, "If you were Abraham's children, you would be doing the works of Abraham. But now you are trying to kill me, a man who has told you the truth that I heard from

God; Abraham did not do this. You are doing the works of your father!" So they said to him, "We were not born of fornication. We have one Father, God." Jesus said to them, "If God were your Father, you would love me, for I came from God and am here; I did not come on my own, but he sent me."

Friends, in today's Gospel, the Lord tells some Jewish listeners that they are enslaved to sin and that the truth will set them free.

Jesus was distinguishing between sins and *sin*, between the underlying disease and its many symptoms. When the Curé d'Ars was asked what wisdom he had gained about human nature from his many years of hearing confessions, he responded, "People are much sadder than they seem." Blaise Pascal rests his apologetic for Christianity on the simple fact that all people are unhappy. This universal, enduring, and stubborn sadness is sin.

Now, this does not mean that sin is identical to psychological depression. The worst sinners can be the most psychologically well-adjusted people, and the greatest saints can be, by any ordinary measure, quite unhappy.

When I speak of sadness in this context, I mean the deep sense of unfulfillment. We want the truth and we get it, if at all, in dribs and drabs; we want the good, and we achieve it only rarely; we seem to know what we ought to be, but we are in fact something else. This spiritual frustration, this inner warfare, this debility of soul, is sin.

Reflect: We are all tainted by the "underlying disease" of sin. What is the connection between our fallen human nature and your own unhappiness or unfulfillment?

APRIL 10, 2025

Thursday of the Fifth Week of Lent

John 8:51–59

Jesus said to the Jews: "Amen, amen, I say to you, whoever keeps my word will never see death." So the Jews said to him, "Now we are sure that you are possessed. Abraham died, as did the prophets, yet you say, 'Whoever keeps my word will never taste death.' Are you greater than our father Abraham, who died? Or the prophets, who died? Who do you make yourself out to be?" Jesus answered, "If I glorify myself, my glory is worth nothing; but it is my Father who glorifies me, of whom you say, 'He is our God.' You do not know him, but I know him. And if I should say that I do not know him, I would be like you a liar. But I do know him and I keep his word. Abraham your father rejoiced to see my day; he saw it and was glad." So the Jews said to him, "You are not yet fifty years old and you have seen Abraham?" Jesus said to them, "Amen, amen, I say to you, before Abraham came to be, I AM." So they picked up stones to throw at him; but Jesus hid and went out of the temple area.

Friends, today, Jesus refers to himself as "I AM," the name God revealed to Moses. So let's reflect on this episode from Exodus. While tending sheep in the hill country, Moses sees a strange sight. There an angel of the Lord appears to him in fire, flaming out of a bush. God sees him and calls him by name: "Moses, Moses! . . . I am the God of your father . . . the God of Abraham, the God of Isaac, and the God of Jacob" (Exod. 3:4, 6). This is a very familiar God, one who knows Moses' ancestors.

Moses makes bold to ask, "When I go to the children of Israel and say to them, 'The God of your fathers has sent me to you,' if they ask me, 'What is his name?' what am I to tell them?" God replies, "I am who I am" (Exod. 3:13–14). What does that mean? God is saying, in essence, "I cannot be defined, described, or delimited. I am not a being, but rather the sheer act of to-be itself."

"This is what you shall tell the children of Israel: I AM sent me to you" (Exod. 3:14). The sheer act of being itself cannot be avoided, and it cannot be controlled. It can only be surrendered to in faith. How shocking and strange Jesus' listeners must have found it when Jesus took this name for himself!

Reflect: How have you tried to avoid or control God, the great I AM?

APRIL 11, 2025

Friday of the Fifth Week of Lent

John 10:31–42

The Jews picked up rocks to stone Jesus. Jesus answered them, "I have shown you many good works from my Father. For which of these are you trying to stone me?" The Jews answered him, "We are not stoning you for a good work but for blasphemy. You, a man, are making yourself God." Jesus answered them, "Is it not written in your law, 'I said, "You are gods"'? If it calls them gods to whom the word of God came, and Scripture cannot be set aside, can you say that the one whom the Father has consecrated and sent into the world blasphemes because I said, 'I am the Son of God'? If I do not perform my Father's works, do not believe me; but if I perform them, even if you do not believe me, believe the works, so that you may realize and understand that the Father is in me and I am in the Father." Then they tried again to arrest him; but he escaped from their power.

He went back across the Jordan to the place where John first baptized, and there he remained. Many came to him and said, "John performed no sign, but everything John said about this man was true." And many there began to believe in him.

Friends, in today's Gospel, Jewish leaders attempt to stone Jesus because he claimed to be the Son of God. He defends his identity, saying, "If I do not perform my Father's works, do not believe me; but if I perform them, even if you do not believe me, believe the works, so that you may realize and understand that the Father is in me and I am in the Father."

At the Last Supper, Jesus would further explain his intimate relationship with the Father. There he lays out for us the coinherence that obtains at the most fundamental dimension of being—that is to say, within the very existence of God. "Master," Philip says to him, "show us the Father, and that will be enough for us." Jesus replies, "Have I been with you for so long a time and you still do not know me, Philip? Whoever has seen me has seen the Father" (John 14:8–9).

How can this be true, unless the Father and the Son coinhere in each other? Though Father and Son are truly distinct, they are utterly implicated in each other by a mutual act of love. As Jesus says, "The Father who dwells in me does his works."

Reflect: What is the difference between following God and participating in his divine life?

APRIL 12, 2025

Saturday of the Fifth Week of Lent

John 11:45–56

Many of the Jews who had come to Mary and seen what Jesus had done began to believe in him. But some of them went to the Pharisees and told them what Jesus had done. So the chief priests and the Pharisees convened the Sanhedrin and said, "What are we going to do? This man is performing many signs. If we leave him alone, all will believe in him, and the Romans will come and take away both our land and our nation." But one of them, Caiaphas, who was high priest that year, said to them, "You know nothing, nor do you consider that it is better for you that one man should die instead of the people, so that the whole nation may not perish." He did not say this on his own, but since he was high priest for that year, he prophesied that Jesus was going to die for the nation, and not only for the nation, but also to gather into one the dispersed children of God. So from that day on they planned to kill him.

So Jesus no longer walked about in public among the Jews, but he left for the region near the desert, to a town called Ephraim, and there he remained with his disciples.

Now the Passover of the Jews was near, and many went up from the country to Jerusalem before Passover to purify themselves. They looked for Jesus and said to one another as they were in the temple area, "What do you think? That he will not come to the feast?"

Friends, in today's Gospel, the chief priests and Pharisees unite in a plot to kill Jesus because he raised Lazarus from the dead.

The Crucifixion of Jesus is a classic instance of Catholic philosopher René Girard's scapegoating theory. He held that a society, large or small, that finds itself in conflict comes together through a common act of blaming an individual or group purportedly responsible for the conflict.

It is utterly consistent with the Girardian theory that Caiaphas, the leading religious figure of the time, said to his colleagues, "It is better for you that one man should die instead of the people, so that the whole nation may not perish."

In any other religious context, this sort of rationalization would be validated. But in the Resurrection of Jesus from the dead, this stunning truth is revealed: God is not on the side of the scapegoaters, but rather on the side of the scapegoated victim.

The true God does not sanction a community created through violence; rather, he sanctions what Jesus called the kingdom of God, a society grounded in forgiveness, love, and identification with the victim.

Reflect: How did the Resurrection turn the scapegoating that Caiaphas supported into the key to our salvation?

APRIL 13, 2025

Palm Sunday of the Passion of the Lord

Luke 22:14–23:56 (or 23:1–49)

When the hour came, Jesus took his place at table with the apostles. He said to them, "I have eagerly desired to eat this Passover with you before I suffer, for, I tell you, I shall not eat it again until there is fulfillment in the kingdom of God." Then he took a cup, gave thanks, and said, "Take this and share it among yourselves; for I tell you that from this time on I shall not drink of the fruit of the vine until the kingdom of God comes." Then he took the bread, said the blessing, broke it, and gave it to them, saying, "This is my body, which will be given for you; do this in memory of me." And likewise the cup after they had eaten, saying, "This cup is the new covenant in my blood, which will be shed for you.

"And yet behold, the hand of the one who is to betray me is with me on the table; for the Son of Man indeed goes as it has been determined; but woe to that man by whom he is betrayed." And they began to debate among themselves who among them would do such a deed.

Then an argument broke out among them about which of them should be regarded as the greatest. He said to them, "The kings of the Gentiles lord it over them and those in authority over them are addressed as 'Benefactors'; but among you it shall not be so. Rather, let the greatest among you be as the youngest, and the leader as the servant. For who is greater: the one seated at table or the one who serves? Is it not the one seated at table? I am among you as the one who serves. It is you who have stood by me in my trials; and I confer a kingdom on you, just as my Father has conferred one on me, that you may eat and drink at my table in my kingdom; and you will sit on thrones judging the twelve tribes of Israel.

"Simon, Simon, behold Satan has demanded to sift all of you like wheat, but I have prayed that your own faith may not fail; and once you have turned back, you must strengthen your brothers." He said to him, "Lord, I am prepared to go to prison and to die with you." But he replied, "I tell you, Peter, before the cock crows this day, you will deny three times that you know me."

He said to them, "When I sent you forth without a money bag or a sack or sandals, were you in need of anything?" "No, nothing," they replied. He said to them, "But now one who has a money bag should take it, and likewise a sack, and one who does not have a sword should sell his cloak and buy one. For I tell you that this Scripture must be fulfilled in me, namely, *He was counted among the wicked*; and indeed what is written about me is coming to fulfillment." Then they said, "Lord, look, there are two swords here." But he replied, "It is enough!"

Then going out, he went, as was his custom, to the Mount of Olives, and the disciples followed him. When he arrived at the place he said to them, "Pray that you may not undergo the test." After withdrawing about a stone's throw from them and kneeling, he prayed, saying, "Father, if you are willing, take this cup away from me; still, not my will but yours be done." And to strengthen him an angel from heaven appeared to him. He was in such agony and he prayed so fervently that his sweat became like drops of blood falling on the ground. When he rose from prayer and returned to his disciples, he found them sleeping from grief. He said to them, "Why are you sleeping? Get up and pray that you may not undergo the test."

While he was still speaking, a crowd approached and in front was one of the Twelve, a man named Judas. He went up to Jesus to kiss him. Jesus said to him, "Judas, are you betraying the Son of Man with a kiss?" His disciples realized what was about to happen, and they asked, "Lord, shall we strike with a sword?" And one of them struck the high priest's servant and cut off his right ear. But Jesus said in reply, "Stop, no more of this!" Then he touched the servant's ear and healed him. And Jesus said to the chief priests and temple guards and elders who had come for him, "Have you come out as against a robber, with swords and clubs? Day after day I was with you in the temple area, and you did not seize me; but this is your hour, the time for the power of darkness."

After arresting him they led him away and took him into the house of the high priest; Peter was following at a distance. They lit a fire in the middle of the courtyard and sat around it, and Peter sat down with them. When a maid saw him seated in the light, she looked intently at him and said, "This man too was with him." But he denied it saying, "Woman, I do not know him." A short while later someone else saw him and said, "You too are one of them"; but Peter answered, "My friend, I am not." About an hour later, still another insisted, "Assuredly, this man too was with him, for he also is a Galilean." But Peter said, "My friend, I do not know what you are talking about." Just as he was saying this, the cock crowed, and the Lord turned and looked at Peter; and Peter remembered the word of the Lord, how he had said to him, "Before the cock crows today, you will deny me three times." He went out and began to weep bitterly. The men who held Jesus in custody were ridiculing and beating him. They blindfolded him and questioned him, saying, "Prophesy! Who is it that struck you?" And they reviled him in saying many other things against him.

When day came the council of elders of the people met, both chief priests and scribes, and they brought him before their Sanhedrin. They said, "If you are the Christ, tell us," but he replied to them, "If I tell you, you will not believe, and if I question, you will not respond. But from this time on the Son of Man will be seated at the right hand of the power of God." They all asked, "Are you then the Son of God?" He replied to them, "You say that I am."

Then they said, "What further need have we for testimony? We have heard it from his own mouth."

Then the whole assembly of them arose and brought him before Pilate. They brought charges against him, saying, "We found this man misleading our people; he opposes the payment of taxes to Caesar and maintains that he is the Christ, a king." Pilate asked him, "Are you the king of the Jews?" He said to him in reply, "You say so." Pilate then addressed the chief priests and the crowds, "I find this man not guilty." But they were adamant and said, "He is inciting the people with his teaching throughout all Judea, from Galilee where he began even to here."

On hearing this Pilate asked if the man was a Galilean; and upon learning that he was under Herod's jurisdiction, he sent him to Herod who was in Jerusalem at that time. Herod was very glad to see Jesus; he had been wanting to see him for a long time, for he had heard about him and had been hoping to see him perform some sign. He questioned him at length, but he gave him no answer. The chief priests and scribes, meanwhile, stood by accusing him harshly. Herod and his soldiers treated him contemptuously and mocked him, and after clothing him in resplendent garb, he sent him back to Pilate. Herod and Pilate became friends that very day, even though they had been enemies formerly. Pilate then summoned the chief priests, the rulers, and the people and said to them, "You brought this man to me and accused him of inciting the people to revolt. I have conducted my investigation in your presence and have not found this man guilty of the charges you have brought against him, nor did Herod, for he sent him back to us. So no capital crime has been committed by him. Therefore I shall have him flogged and then release him."

But all together they shouted out, "Away with this man! Release Barabbas to us."—Now Barabbas had been imprisoned for a rebellion that had taken place in the city and for murder.—Again Pilate addressed them, still wishing to release Jesus, but they continued their shouting, "Crucify him! Crucify him!" Pilate addressed them a third time, "What evil has this man done? I found him guilty of no capital crime. Therefore I shall have him flogged and then release him." With loud shouts, however, they persisted in calling for his crucifixion, and their voices prevailed. The verdict of Pilate was that their demand should be granted. So he released the man who had been imprisoned for rebellion and murder, for whom they asked, and he handed Jesus over to them to deal with as they wished.

As they led him away they took hold of a certain Simon, a Cyrenian, who was coming in from the country; and after laying the cross on him, they made him carry it behind Jesus. A large crowd of people followed Jesus, including many women who mourned and lamented him. Jesus turned to them and said, "Daughters of Jerusalem, do not weep for me; weep instead for yourselves and for your children for indeed, the days are coming when people will say, 'Blessed are the barren, the wombs that never bore and the breasts that never nursed.' At that time people will say to the mountains, 'Fall upon us!' and to the hills, 'Cover us!' for if these things are done when the wood is green what will happen when it is dry?" Now two others, both criminals, were led away with him to be executed.

When they came to the place called the Skull, they crucified him and the criminals there, one on his right, the other on his left. Then Jesus said, "Father, forgive them, they know not what they do." They divided his garments by casting lots. The people stood by and watched; the rulers, meanwhile, sneered at him and said, "He saved others, let him save himself if he is the chosen one, the Christ of God." Even the soldiers jeered at him. As they approached to offer him wine they called out, "If you are King of the Jews, save yourself." Above him there was an inscription that read, "This is the King of the Jews."

Now one of the criminals hanging there reviled Jesus, saying, "Are you not the Christ? Save yourself and us." The other, however, rebuking him, said in reply, "Have you no fear of God, for you are subject to the same condemnation? And indeed, we have been condemned justly, for the sentence we received corresponds to our crimes, but this man has done nothing criminal." Then he said, "Jesus, remember me when you come into your kingdom." He replied to him, "Amen, I say to you, today you will be with me in Paradise."

It was now about noon and darkness came over the whole land until three in the afternoon because of an eclipse of the sun. Then the veil of the temple was torn down the middle. Jesus cried out in a loud voice, "Father, into your hands I commend my spirit"; and when he had said this he breathed his last.

Here all kneel and pause for a short time.

The centurion who witnessed what had happened glorified God and said, "This man was innocent beyond doubt." When all the people who had gathered for this spectacle saw what had happened, they returned home beating their breasts; but all his acquaintances stood at a distance, including the women who had followed him from Galilee and saw these events.

Now there was a virtuous and righteous man named Joseph who, though he was a member of the council, had not consented to their plan of action. He came from the Jewish town of Arimathea and was awaiting the kingdom of God. He went to Pilate and asked for the body of Jesus. After he had taken the body down, he wrapped it in a linen cloth and laid him in a rock-hewn tomb in which no one had yet been buried. It was the day of preparation, and the sabbath was about to begin. The women who had come from Galilee with him followed behind, and when they had seen the tomb and the way in which his body was laid in it, they returned and prepared spices and perfumed oils. Then they rested on the sabbath according to the commandment.

Friends, how dark are the readings for Palm Sunday! We read through Luke's Passion narrative, leaving out the good news of the Resurrection. To get to the bottom of this emphasis on suffering, to decipher its religious meaning, is to uncover the theological significance of this day.

Do you remember the first time that life really knocked you around? It might have been an extraordinary failure; it might have been the first time you confronted real violence or real hatred; it might have been a massive disappointment; it might have been the death of someone that you loved. This mess, this problem, bedevils all of us.

The biblical approach is clear: God sets about a rescue operation—the formation of a holy people Israel who would follow his commands, worship him aright, and thereby become a magnet to the world. They would teach and show the way out of the dilemma.

He would form a people ready to receive him; he would gradually effect a unity between divinity and humanity; and one day, a servant of Yahweh would appear, someone despised and reviled by men. And this mysterious figure would solve the problem by bearing away the sins of the world, by carrying them off through his suffering.

Reflect: Reflect on the marvel of God's plan of salvation and how he turns suffering into triumph for all who believe.

APRIL 14, 2025

Monday of Holy Week

John 12:1–11

Six days before Passover Jesus came to Bethany, where Lazarus was, whom Jesus had raised from the dead. They gave a dinner for him there, and Martha served, while Lazarus was one of those reclining at table with him. Mary took a liter of costly perfumed oil made from genuine aromatic nard and anointed the feet of Jesus and dried them with her hair; the house was filled with the fragrance of the oil. Then Judas the Iscariot, one of his disciples, and the one who would betray him, said, "Why was this oil not sold for three hundred days' wages and given to the poor?" He said this not because he cared about the poor but because he was a thief and held the money bag and used to steal the contributions. So Jesus said, "Leave her alone. Let her keep this for the day of my burial. You always have the poor with you, but you do not always have me."

The large crowd of the Jews found out that he was there and came, not only because of him, but also to see Lazarus, whom he had raised from the dead. And the chief priests plotted to kill Lazarus too, because many of the Jews were turning away and believing in Jesus because of him.

Friends, in today's Gospel, Mary of Bethany anoints Jesus' feet with perfumed oil, preparing him for burial.

This gesture—wasting something as expensive as an entire jar of perfume—is sniffed at by Judas, who complains that, at the very least, the nard could have been sold and the money given to the poor.

Why does John use this tale to preface his telling of the Passion? Why does he allow the odor of this woman's perfume to waft, as it were, over the whole of the story? It is because, I believe, this extravagant gesture shows forth the meaning of what Jesus is about to do: the absolutely radical giving away of self.

There is nothing calculating, careful, or conservative about the woman's action. Flowing from the deepest place in the heart, religion resists the strictures set for it by a fussily moralizing reason (on full display in Judas' complaint about the woman's extravagance). At the climax of his life, Jesus will give himself away totally, lavishly, unreasonably—and this is why Mary's beautiful gesture is a sort of overture to the opera that will follow.

Reflect: When have you been the giver or the recipient of an extravagant gesture of love? How did that affect you?

APRIL 15, 2025

Tuesday of Holy Week

John 13:21–33, 36–38

Reclining at table with his disciples, Jesus was deeply troubled and testified, "Amen, amen, I say to you, one of you will betray me." The disciples looked at one another, at a loss as to whom he meant. One of his disciples, the one whom Jesus loved, was reclining at Jesus' side. So Simon Peter nodded to him to find out whom he meant. He leaned back against Jesus' chest and said to him, "Master, who is it?" Jesus answered, "It is the one to whom I hand the morsel after I have dipped it." So he dipped the morsel and took it and handed it to Judas, son of Simon the Iscariot. After Judas took the morsel, Satan entered him. So Jesus said to him, "What you are going to do, do quickly." Now none of those reclining at table realized why he said this to him. Some thought that since Judas kept the money bag, Jesus had told him, "Buy what we need for the feast," or to give something to the poor. So Judas took the morsel and left at once. And it was night.

When he had left, Jesus said, "Now is the Son of Man glorified, and God is glorified in him. If God is glorified in him, God will also glorify him in himself, and he will glorify him at once. My children, I will be with you only a little while longer. You will look for me, and as I told the Jews, 'Where I go you cannot come,' so now I say it to you."

Simon Peter said to him, "Master, where are you going?" Jesus answered him, "Where I am going, you cannot follow me now, though you will follow later." Peter said to him, "Master, why can I not follow you now? I will lay down my life for you." Jesus answered, "Will you lay down your life for me? Amen, amen, I say to you, the cock will not crow before you deny me three times."

Friends, in today's Gospel, Jesus foretells the denial of Peter, which is fulfilled in the account of the Passion. Peter later denies Jesus three times before the cock crows and, remembering Jesus' prediction, breaks down and weeps.

After the Resurrection, Peter and the other disciples return to Galilee to work as fishermen again, and there spot Jesus on the far shore. As Jesus draws Peter back into his circle of intimacy, we witness a beautiful act of spiritual direction. Three times the Lord asks Peter whether he loves him, and three times Peter affirms it: "Lord, you know that I love you" (John 21:15).

St. Augustine commented that the threefold statement of love was meant to counteract the threefold denial. Peter emerges as the archetype of the forgiven and commissioned Church, for after each of his reaffirmations, Peter hears the command to tend the sheep. Once we are brought back into friendship with Jesus, we are called to love those whom he loves.

Reflect: Reflect on this and other Gospel stories about Peter. In what ways is he an appropriate archetype of the Church?

APRIL 16, 2025

Wednesday of Holy Week

Matthew 26:14–25

One of the Twelve, who was called Judas Iscariot, went to the chief priests and said, "What are you willing to give me if I hand him over to you?" They paid him thirty pieces of silver, and from that time on he looked for an opportunity to hand him over.

On the first day of the Feast of Unleavened Bread, the disciples approached Jesus and said, "Where do you want us to prepare for you to eat the Passover?" He said, "Go into the city to a certain man and tell him, 'The teacher says, My appointed time draws near; in your house I shall celebrate the Passover with my disciples.'" The disciples then did as Jesus had ordered, and prepared the Passover.

When it was evening, he reclined at table with the Twelve. And while they were eating, he said, "Amen, I say to you, one of you will betray me." Deeply distressed at this, they began to say to him one after another, "Surely it is not I, Lord?" He said in reply, "He who has dipped his hand into the dish with me is the one who will betray me. The Son of Man indeed goes, as it is written of him, but woe to that man by whom the Son of Man is betrayed. It would be better for that man if he had never been born." Then Judas, his betrayer, said in reply, "Surely it is not I, Rabbi?" He answered, "You have said so."

Friends, in today's Gospel, the Lord identifies Judas as his betrayer. And after this he performs his greatest wonder.

In the course of the supper, Jesus identifies himself so radically with the Passover bread and wine that they become his Body and his Blood. Like broken bread, the Lord says, his body will be given away in love; and like spilled wine, his blood will be poured out on behalf of many.

How does this terrible gathering come to a close? They sing! Matthew tells us, "When they had sung the hymn, they went out to the Mount of Olives." Can you imagine a condemned criminal blithely singing on the eve of his execution? Wouldn't there be something odd, even macabre, about such a display?

But Jesus knows—and his Church knows with him—that this joyful outburst, precisely at that awful time, is altogether appropriate. This is not to deny for a moment the terror of that night nor the seriousness of what will follow the next day; but it is to acknowledge that an act of total love is the passage to fullness of life.

Reflect: How does partaking in the Body and Blood of Jesus at Mass affect you?

APRIL 17, 2025

Holy Thursday (Evening Mass of the Lord's Supper)

John 13:1–15

Before the feast of Passover, Jesus knew that his hour had come to pass from this world to the Father. He loved his own in the world and he loved them to the end. The devil had already induced Judas, son of Simon the Iscariot, to hand him over. So, during supper, fully aware that the Father had put everything into his power and that he had come from God and was returning to God, he rose from supper and took off his outer garments. He took a towel and tied it around his waist. Then he poured water into a basin and began to wash the disciples' feet and dry them with the towel around his waist. He came to Simon Peter, who said to him, "Master, are you going to wash my feet?" Jesus answered and said to him, "What I am doing, you do not understand now, but you will understand later." Peter said to him, "You will never wash my feet." Jesus answered him, "Unless I wash you, you will have no inheritance with me." Simon Peter said to him, "Master, then not only my feet, but my hands and head as well." Jesus said to him, "Whoever has bathed has no need except to have his feet washed, for he is clean all over; so you are clean, but not all." For he knew who would betray him; for this reason, he said, "Not all of you are clean."

So when he had washed their feet and put his garments back on and reclined at table again, he said to them, "Do you realize what I have done for you? You call me 'teacher' and 'master,' and rightly so, for indeed I am. If I, therefore, the master and teacher, have washed your feet, you ought to wash one another's feet. I have given you a model to follow, so that as I have done for you, you should also do."

Friends, in today's Gospel, Jesus gathers with his chosen twelve at the climax of his life and does something so strange that we still wonder at it two thousand years later: he takes off his outer garment, puts a towel around his waist, and begins to wash his disciples' feet.

The nineteenth-century philosopher Hegel said that all human society, to varying degrees, is characterized by the master-slave dynamic. Long before Hegel, the great St. Augustine noticed what he called the *libido dominandi*, the "lust to dominate," as the mark of a dysfunctional society. Long before Augustine, the authors of the Old Testament were also interested in this problem, because the central story of the Scriptures is that of slavery and liberation from slavery—the Passover event.

But we see now in John's Gospel how the distinctive mark of Jesus' kingdom is precisely the overturning of the master-slave dynamic. Jesus bends down to do the work that was so lowly and frankly gross that only the lowest of the slaves were expected to do it, and he says, "As I have done for you, you should also do." And what does he do later at the same supper? He gives himself away entirely in the Eucharist: "This is my body, which will be given for you" (Luke 22:19).

It is into this new dynamic that we are invited by Jesus: the washing of the feet, the giving away of body and blood.

Reflect: How can you imitate this radical dynamic in a concrete way today?

APRIL 18, 2025

Friday of the Passion of the Lord (Good Friday)

John 18:1–19:42

Jesus went out with his disciples across the Kidron valley to where there was a garden, into which he and his disciples entered. Judas his betrayer also knew the place, because Jesus had often met there with his disciples. So Judas got a band of soldiers and guards from the chief priests and the Pharisees and went there with lanterns, torches, and weapons. Jesus, knowing everything that was going to happen to him, went out and said to them, "Whom are you looking for?" They answered him, "Jesus the Nazorean." He said to them, "I AM." Judas his betrayer was also with them. When he said to them, "I AM," they turned away and fell to the ground. So he again asked them, "Whom are you looking for?" They said, "Jesus the Nazorean." Jesus answered, "I told you that I AM. So if you are looking for me, let these men go." This was to fulfill what he had said, "I have not lost any of those you gave me." Then Simon Peter, who had a sword, drew it, struck the high priest's slave, and cut off his right ear. The slave's name was Malchus. Jesus said to Peter, "Put your sword into its scabbard. Shall I not drink the cup that the Father gave me?"

So the band of soldiers, the tribune, and the Jewish guards seized Jesus, bound him, and brought him to Annas first. He was the father-in-law of Caiaphas, who was high priest that year. It was Caiaphas who had counseled the Jews that it was better that one man should die rather than the people.

Simon Peter and another disciple followed Jesus. Now the other disciple was known to the high priest, and he entered the courtyard of the high priest with Jesus. But Peter stood at the gate outside. So the other disciple, the acquaintance of the high priest, went out and spoke to the gatekeeper and brought Peter in. Then the maid who was the gatekeeper said to Peter, "You are not one of this man's disciples, are you?" He said, "I am not." Now the slaves and the guards were standing around a charcoal fire that they had made, because it was cold, and were warming themselves. Peter was also standing there keeping warm.

The high priest questioned Jesus about his disciples and about his doctrine. Jesus answered him, "I have spoken publicly to the world. I have always taught in a synagogue or in the temple area where all the Jews gather, and in secret I have said nothing. Why ask me? Ask those who heard me what I said to them. They know what I said." When he had said this, one of the temple guards standing there struck Jesus and said, "Is this the way you answer the high priest?" Jesus answered him, "If I have spoken wrongly, testify to the wrong; but if I have spoken rightly, why do you strike me?" Then Annas sent him bound to Caiaphas the high priest.

Now Simon Peter was standing there keeping warm. And they said to him, "You are not one of his disciples, are you?" He denied it and said, "I am not." One of the slaves of the high priest, a relative of the one whose ear Peter had cut off, said, "Didn't I see you in the garden with him?" Again Peter denied it. And immediately the cock crowed.

Then they brought Jesus from Caiaphas to the praetorium. It was morning. And they themselves did not enter the praetorium, in order not to be defiled so that they could eat the Passover. So Pilate came out to them and said, "What charge do you bring against this man?" They answered and said to him, "If he were not a criminal, we would not have handed him over to you." At this, Pilate said to them, “Take him yourselves, and judge him according to your law.” The Jews answered him, “We do not have the right to execute anyone,” in order that the word of Jesus might be fulfilled that he said indicating the kind of death he would die. So Pilate went back into the praetorium and summoned Jesus and said to him, “Are you the King of the Jews?” Jesus answered, “Do you say this on your own or have others told you about me?” Pilate answered, “I am not a Jew, am I? Your own nation and the chief priests handed you over to me. What have you done?” Jesus answered, “My kingdom does not belong to this world. If my kingdom did belong to this world, my attendants would be fighting to keep me from being handed over to the Jews. But as it is, my kingdom is not here.” So Pilate said to him, “Then you are a king?” Jesus answered, “You say I am a king. For this I was born and for this I came into the world, to testify to the truth. Everyone who belongs to the truth listens to my voice.” Pilate said to him, “What is truth?”

When he had said this, he again went out to the Jews and said to them, “I find no guilt in him. But you have a custom that I release one prisoner to you at Passover. Do you want me to release to you the King of the Jews?" They cried out again, "Not this one but Barabbas!" Now Barabbas was a revolutionary.

Then Pilate took Jesus and had him scourged. And the soldiers wove a crown out of thorns and placed it on his head, and clothed him in a purple cloak, and they came to him and said, "Hail, King of the Jews!" And they struck him repeatedly. Once more Pilate went out and said to them, "Look, I am bringing him out to you, so that you may know that I find no guilt in him." So Jesus came out, wearing the crown of thorns and the purple cloak. And he said to them, "Behold, the man!" When the chief priests and the guards saw him they cried out, "Crucify him, crucify him!" Pilate said to them, "Take him yourselves and crucify him. I find no guilt in him." The Jews answered, "We have a law, and according to that law he ought to die, because he made himself the Son of God." Now when Pilate heard this statement, he became even more afraid, and went back into the praetorium and said to Jesus, "Where are you from?" Jesus did not answer him. So Pilate said to him, "Do you not speak to me? Do you not know that I have power to release you and I have power to crucify you?" Jesus answered him, "You would have no power over me if it had not been given to you from above. For this reason the one who handed me over to you has the greater sin." Consequently, Pilate tried to release him; but the Jews cried out, "If you release him, you are not a Friend of Caesar. Everyone who makes himself a king opposes Caesar."

When Pilate heard these words he brought Jesus out and seated him on the judge's bench in the place called Stone Pavement, in Hebrew, Gabbatha. It was preparation day for Passover, and it was about noon. And he said to the Jews, "Behold, your king!" They cried out, "Take him away, take him away! Crucify him!" Pilate said to them, "Shall I crucify your king?" The chief priests answered, "We have no king but Caesar." Then he handed him over to them to be crucified.

So they took Jesus, and, carrying the cross himself, he went out to what is called the Place of the Skull, in Hebrew, Golgotha. There they crucified him, and with him two others, one on either side, with Jesus in the middle. Pilate also had an inscription written and put on the cross. It read, "Jesus the Nazorean, the King of the Jews." Now many of the Jews read this inscription, because the place where Jesus was crucified was near the city; and it was written in Hebrew, Latin, and Greek. So the chief priests of the Jews said to Pilate, "Do not write 'The King of the Jews,' but that he said, 'I am the King of the Jews.'" Pilate answered, "What I have written, I have written."

When the soldiers had crucified Jesus, they took his clothes and divided them into four shares, a share for each soldier. They also took his tunic, but the tunic was seamless, woven in one piece from the top down. So they said to one another, "Let's not tear it, but cast lots for it to see whose it will be," in order that the passage of Scripture might be fulfilled that says:

They divided my garments among them,
and for my vesture they cast lots.

This is what the soldiers did. Standing by the cross of Jesus were his mother and his mother's sister, Mary the wife of Clopas, and Mary of Magdala. When Jesus saw his mother and the disciple there whom he loved he said to his mother, "Woman, behold, your son." Then he said to the disciple, "Behold, your mother." And from that hour the disciple took her into his home.

After this, aware that everything was now finished, in order that the Scripture might be fulfilled, Jesus said, "I thirst." There was a vessel filled with common wine. So they put a sponge soaked in wine on a sprig of hyssop and put it up to his mouth. When Jesus had taken the wine, he said, "It is finished." And bowing his head, he handed over the spirit.

Here all kneel and pause for a short time.

Now since it was preparation day, in order that the bodies might not remain on the cross on the sabbath, for the sabbath day of that week was a solemn one, the Jews asked Pilate that their legs be broken and that they be taken down. So the soldiers came and broke the legs of the first and then of the other one who was crucified with Jesus. But when they came to Jesus and saw that he was already dead, they did not break his legs, but one soldier thrust his lance into his side, and immediately blood and water flowed out. An eyewitness has testified, and his testimony is true; he knows that he is speaking the truth, so that you also may come to believe. For this happened so that the Scripture passage might be fulfilled:

Not a bone of it will be broken.

And again another passage says:

They will look upon him whom they have pierced.

After this, Joseph of Arimathea, secretly a disciple of Jesus for fear of the Jews, asked Pilate if he could remove the body of Jesus. And Pilate permitted it. So he came and took his body. Nicodemus, the one who had first come to him at night, also came bringing a mixture of myrrh and aloes weighing about one hundred pounds. They took the body of Jesus and bound it with burial cloths along with the spices, according to the Jewish burial custom. Now in the place where he had been crucified there was a garden, and in the garden a new tomb, in which no one had yet been buried. So they laid Jesus there because of the Jewish preparation day; for the tomb was close by.

Friends, today's Gospel is John's wonderful narrative of Christ's Passion.

On the cross, Jesus entered into close quarters with sin (because that's where we sinners are found) and allowed the heat and fury of sin to destroy him, even as he protected us.

We can see, with special clarity, why the first Christians associated the crucified Jesus with the suffering servant of Isaiah. By enduring the pain of the cross, Jesus did indeed bear our sins; by his stripes we were indeed healed.

And this is why the sacrificial death of Jesus is pleasing to the Father. The Father sent his Son into godforsakenness, into the morass of sin and death—not because he delighted in seeing his Son suffer, but rather because he wanted his Son to bring the divine light to the darkest place.

It is not the agony of the Son in itself that pleases his Father, but rather the Son's willing obedience in offering his body in sacrifice in order to take away the sin of the world. St. Anselm said that the death of the Son reestablished the right relationship between divinity and humanity.

Reflect: Why does the sacrificial death of Jesus on the cross showcase the greatest love?

APRIL 19, 2025

Holy Saturday (Easter Vigil)

Luke 24:1–12

At daybreak on the first day of the week the women who had come from Galilee with Jesus took the spices they had prepared and went to the tomb. They found the stone rolled away from the tomb; but when they entered, they did not find the body of the Lord Jesus. While they were puzzling over this, behold, two men in dazzling garments appeared to them. They were terrified and bowed their faces to the ground. They said to them, "Why do you seek the living one among the dead? He is not here, but he has been raised. Remember what he said to you while he was still in Galilee, that the Son of Man must be handed over to sinners and be crucified, and rise on the third day." And they remembered his words. Then they returned from the tomb and announced all these things to the eleven and to all the others. The women were Mary Magdalene, Joanna, and Mary the mother of James; the others who accompanied them also told this to the apostles, but their story seemed like nonsense and they did not believe them. But Peter got up and ran to the tomb, bent down, and saw the burial cloths alone; then he went home amazed at what had happened.

Friends, how wonderful are the readings for the Easter season! So full of theological depth, so spiritually rich, so marked by joy.

In light of the Resurrection, we know that God's deepest intention for us is life, and life to the full. He does not want death to have the final word; he wants a renewal of the heavens and the earth.

Therefore, we have to stop living in the intellectual and spiritual space of death. We have to stop living intellectually in a world dominated by death and the fear of death. We have to adjust our attitudes in order to respond properly to what God really intends for us and the world.

Though we rarely admit it, we live in a death-haunted space. The fear of death broods over us like a cloud and conditions all of our thoughts and actions. What if we really believed, deep down, that death did not have the final word? Would we live in such fear, in such a cramped spiritual space? Or would we see that the protection of our egos is not the number one concern of our existence?

Reflect: How do you honestly feel about your own death? Do you succumb to the culture's way of ignoring death? Do you fear death?

APRIL 20, 2025

Easter Sunday of the Resurrection of the Lord

John 20:1–9 (or Luke 24:1–12)

On the first day of the week, Mary of Magdala came to the tomb early in the morning, while it was still dark, and saw the stone removed from the tomb. So she ran and went to Simon Peter and to the other disciple whom Jesus loved, and told them, "They have taken the Lord from the tomb, and we don't know where they put him." So Peter and the other disciple went out and came to the tomb. They both ran, but the other disciple ran faster than Peter and arrived at the tomb first; he bent down and saw the burial cloths there, but did not go in. When Simon Peter arrived after him, he went into the tomb and saw the burial cloths there, and the cloth that had covered his head, not with the burial cloths but rolled up in a separate place. Then the other disciple also went in, the one who had arrived at the tomb first, and he saw and believed. For they did not yet understand the Scripture that he had to rise from the dead.

Friends, our Easter Gospel contains St. John's magnificent account of the Resurrection. It was, says John, early in the morning on the first day of the week. It was still dark—just the way it was at the beginning of time before God said "Let there be light" (Gen. 1:3). But a light was about to shine, and a new creation was about to appear.

The stone had been rolled away. That stone, blocking entrance to the tomb of Jesus, stands for the finality of death. When someone whom we love dies, it is as though a great stone is rolled across them, permanently blocking our access to them. And this is why we weep at death—not just in grief but in a kind of existential frustration.

But for Jesus, the stone had been rolled away. Undoubtedly, the first disciples must have thought a grave robber had been at work. But the wonderful Johannine irony is that the greatest of grave robbers had indeed been at work. The Lord says to the prophet Ezekiel, "I am going to open your graves, and bring you up from your graves."

What was dreamed about, what endured as a hope against hope, has become a reality. God has opened the grave of his Son, and the bonds of death have been shattered forever.

Reflect: How does the Resurrection imbue your daily life with hope?

CONCLUSION

Friends,

In the name of the risen Lord, greetings! Lent is over and we've now moved into Easter. Alleluia!

I'd like to thank you for joining me on this journey through the Lenten season. Now that we've finished, you might be wondering, what's next? How do I maintain the spiritual momentum I developed during Lent? I'd like to suggest a few practical tips.

First, be sure to visit our website, wordonfire.org, on a regular basis. There you'll find lots of helpful resources, including new articles, videos, podcasts, and homilies, all designed to help strengthen your faith and evangelize the culture. The best part is that all of it is free!

In addition to those free resources, I invite you to join the Word on Fire Institute. This is an online hub of deep spiritual and intellectual formation, where you'll journey through courses taught by me and other professors. Our goal is to build an army of evangelists, people who have been transformed by Christ and want to bring his light to the world. Learn more and sign up at wordonfire.institute.

Finally, consider carrying on your Lenten progress by grounding your life more concretely in the Eucharist, which is what keeps us alive spiritually. Are you only attending Mass on Sundays? Commit to attending one extra Mass each week. Is there a chapel nearby that offers Eucharistic Adoration? Sign up for a weekly hour of meditation and prayer before the Blessed Sacrament. The Eucharist is the alpha and the omega of Christian discipleship. It is the energy without which authentic Christianity runs down.

Again, thank you from all of us at Word on Fire, and God bless you during this Easter season!

Peace,

+Robert Barron

Bishop Robert Barron

THE STATIONS OF

THE CROSS

Visit wordonfire.org/stations/ for
the Stations of the Cross with Bishop Barron.

All Stations of the Cross images are from the Church of All Saints in Blato, Korcula Island, Croatia.

OPENING PRAYER

In the name of the Father, and of the Son, and of the Holy Spirit.
Amen.

℣. Lord Jesus Christ, Son of God,
℟. Have mercy on me, a sinner.
℣. Lord Jesus Christ, Son of God,
℟. Have mercy on me, a sinner.
℣. Lord Jesus Christ, Son of God,
℟. Have mercy on me, a sinner.

The First Station

JESUS IS CONDEMNED TO DEATH

℣. We adore you, O Christ, and we bless you.
(Genuflect)
℟. Because by your holy cross you have redeemed the world.
(Rise)

Leader: Jesus stands before Pontius Pilate, the local representative of Caesar. Pilate, undoubtedly sure of his worldly power and authority, sizes up this criminal, asking, "Are you the King of the Jews?" Jesus responds, "My kingdom does not belong to this world. . . . For this I came into the world, to testify to the truth." Unimpressed, Pilate asks, "What is truth?" And then he condemns Jesus to death. *(Kneel)*

All pray: Lord Jesus, Israel dreamed of a new King who would defeat its enemies and reign over the whole world. You accomplished this through your cross and Resurrection, outmaneuvering the sin of the world and swallowing it up in the divine forgiveness. Help us to give our full allegiance to you each day, rejecting the old reign of violence and power and embracing your reign of nonviolence and love.

(Optional)

Our Father, who art in heaven,
hallowed be thy name;
thy kingdom come,
thy will be done
on earth as it is in heaven.
Give us this day our daily bread,
and forgive us our trespasses,
as we forgive those who trespass against us;
and lead us not into temptation,
but deliver us from evil.
Amen.

Hail Mary, full of grace, the Lord is with thee;
blessed art thou among women,
and blessed is the fruit of thy womb, Jesus.
Holy Mary, Mother of God,
pray for us sinners,
now and at the hour of our death.
Amen.

Glory be to the Father, and to the Son, and to the Holy Spirit; as it was in the beginning, is now, and ever shall be, world without end.
Amen.

(Rise)

All sing:

Stabat Mater dolorosa
Iuxta Crucem lacrimosa,
Dum pendebat Filius.

At the cross her station keeping,
Stood the mournful Mother weeping,
Close to Jesus to the last.

The Second Station

JESUS TAKES UP HIS CROSS

℣. We adore you, O Christ, and we bless you.
(Genuflect)
℟. Because by your holy cross you have redeemed the world.
(Rise)

Leader: God the Father sends his Son to the cross—not out of anger, but out of love; not to see him suffer, but to set things right. "For God so loved the world that he gave his only Son, so that everyone who believes in him might not perish but might have eternal life." God the Son willingly takes up that terrible cross—a sacrifice expressive of compassion for us sinners.
(Kneel)

All pray: Lord Jesus, you took up the cross; give us the grace to take up our cross daily and follow you. You lived in self forgetting love unto death; give us the grace to be such love. You broke open your own heart for us; give us the grace to open our hearts for others.

(Optional)

Our Father, who art in heaven,
hallowed be thy name;
thy kingdom come,
thy will be done
on earth as it is in heaven.
Give us this day our daily bread,
and forgive us our trespasses,
as we forgive those who trespass against us;
and lead us not into temptation,
but deliver us from evil.
Amen.

Hail Mary, full of grace, the Lord is with thee;
blessed art thou among women,
and blessed is the fruit of thy womb, Jesus.
Holy Mary, Mother of God,
pray for us sinners,
now and at the hour of our death.
Amen.

Glory be to the Father, and to the Son, and to the Holy Spirit; as it was in the beginning, is now, and ever shall be, world without end.
Amen.

(Rise)

All sing:

Cuius animam gementem,
Contristatam et dolentem,
Pertransivit gladius.

Through her heart, his sorrow sharing,
All his bitter anguish bearing,
Now at length the sword had passed.

The Third Station

JESUS FALLS FOR THE FIRST TIME

℣. We adore you, O Christ, and we bless you.
(Genuflect)
℟. Because by your holy cross you have redeemed the world.
(Rise)

Leader: Jesus—crowned with thorns and already almost drained of blood—is made to carry his cross. As he makes his painful way to Calvary, bearing the burdens of the world's sin, he falls under the tremendous weight.
(Kneel)

All pray: Lord Jesus, we so often see the universe as turning around our egos and needs. Rescue us from the insanity of sin, which brings about spiritual disintegration and death. As you bore our burdens, disempowering them from within, may we actively lower ourselves to bear the burdens of others.

(Optional)

Our Father, who art in heaven,
hallowed be thy name;
thy kingdom come,
thy will be done
on earth as it is in heaven.
Give us this day our daily bread,
and forgive us our trespasses,
as we forgive those who trespass against us;
and lead us not into temptation,
but deliver us from evil.
Amen.

Hail Mary, full of grace, the Lord is with thee;
blessed art thou among women,
and blessed is the fruit of thy womb, Jesus.
Holy Mary, Mother of God,
pray for us sinners,
now and at the hour of our death.
Amen.

Glory be to the Father, and to the Son, and to the Holy Spirit; as it was in the beginning, is now, and ever shall be, world without end.
Amen.

(Rise)

All sing:

O quam tristis et afflicta
Fuit illa benedicta
Mater Unigeniti!

Oh, how sad and sore distressed
Was that Mother highly blest
Of the sole-begotten One!

The Fourth Station

JESUS MEETS HIS BLESSED MOTHER

℣. We adore you, O Christ, and we bless you.
(Genuflect)
℟. Because by your holy cross you have redeemed the world.
(Rise)

Leader: As he carries the cross, Jesus meets his Blessed Mother, the Virgin Mary. The humble handmaid through whom Christ was born now watches him approach his death, a sword of sorrow piercing her soul.
(Kneel)

All pray: Holy Mary, you followed your son all the way to the cross, where he entrusted us to you as our mother and the privileged channel of his grace. Intercede for us, that we might be drawn into deeper fellowship with him.

(Optional)

Our Father, who art in heaven,
hallowed be thy name;
thy kingdom come,
thy will be done
on earth as it is in heaven.
Give us this day our daily bread,
and forgive us our trespasses,
as we forgive those who trespass against us;
and lead us not into temptation,
but deliver us from evil.
Amen.

Hail Mary, full of grace, the Lord is with thee;
blessed art thou among women,
and blessed is the fruit of thy womb, Jesus.
Holy Mary, Mother of God,
pray for us sinners,
now and at the hour of our death.
Amen.

Glory be to the Father, and to the Son, and to the Holy Spirit; as it was in the beginning, is now, and ever shall be, world without end.
Amen.

(Rise)

All sing:

Quae moerebat, et dolebat,
Pia Mater, dum videbat
Nati poenas inclyti.

Christ above in torment hangs;
She beneath beholds the pangs
Of her dying glorious Son.

The Fifth Station

SIMON OF CYRENE IS MADE TO HELP JESUS BEAR THE CROSS

℣. We adore you, O Christ, and we bless you.
(Genuflect)
℟. Because by your holy cross you have redeemed the world.
(Rise)

Leader: The Romans, not wanting Christ to die before his Crucifixion, press into service Simon of Cyrene. How perilous and dangerous this must have seemed to Simon! But he seizes the moment and helps Jesus with the cross, bearing some of his suffering.
(Kneel)

All pray: Lord Jesus, at the moment of truth, Simon of Cyrene saw that you had need of him—and he responded. Help us, too, to see and respond to your need of us. Even if we are unnoticed or mocked, press us into service to bear you into the world.

(Optional)

Our Father, who art in heaven,
hallowed be thy name;
thy kingdom come,
thy will be done
on earth as it is in heaven.
Give us this day our daily bread,
and forgive us our trespasses,
as we forgive those who trespass against us;
and lead us not into temptation,
but deliver us from evil.
Amen.

Hail Mary, full of grace, the Lord is with thee;
blessed art thou among women,
and blessed is the fruit of thy womb, Jesus.
Holy Mary, Mother of God,
pray for us sinners,
now and at the hour of our death.
Amen.

Glory be to the Father, and to the Son, and to the Holy Spirit; as it was in the beginning, is now, and ever shall be, world without end.
Amen.

(Rise)

All sing:

Quis est homo qui non fleret,
Matrem Christi si videret
In tanto supplicio?

Is there one who would not weep,
Whelmed in miseries so deep
Christ's dear Mother to behold?

The Sixth Station

VERONICA WIPES THE FACE OF JESUS

℣. We adore you, O Christ, and we bless you.
(Genuflect)
℟. Because by your holy cross you have redeemed the world.
(Rise)

Leader: A woman called Veronica approaches and wipes the blood and sweat from Jesus' face as he continues his way to Calvary. An image of the face of Christ—the divine Word made flesh—is miraculously imprinted on her veil.
(Kneel)

All pray: Lord Jesus, in your Holy Face, we see the ugliness of our sin, which rules out our self-justification. But we also see the face of mercy, which lifts us from our self-reproach. In your agonies, you reveal our agony and take it away. Keep our gaze fixed on yours, and strengthen us in our mission of drawing the whole world toward you.

(Optional)

Our Father, who art in heaven,
hallowed be thy name;
thy kingdom come,
thy will be done
on earth as it is in heaven.
Give us this day our daily bread,
and forgive us our trespasses,
as we forgive those who trespass against us;
and lead us not into temptation,
but deliver us from evil.
Amen.

Hail Mary, full of grace, the Lord is with thee;
blessed art thou among women,
and blessed is the fruit of thy womb, Jesus.
Holy Mary, Mother of God,
pray for us sinners,
now and at the hour of our death.
Amen.

Glory be to the Father, and to the Son, and to the Holy Spirit; as it was in the beginning, is now, and ever shall be, world without end.
Amen.

(Rise)

All sing:

Quis non posset contristari
Christi Matrem contemplari
Dolentem cum Filio?

Can the human heart refrain
From partaking in her pain,
In that Mother's pain untold?

The Seventh Station

JESUS FALLS FOR THE SECOND TIME

℣. We adore you, O Christ, and we bless you.
(Genuflect)
℟. Because by your holy cross you have redeemed the world.
(Rise)

Leader: Under the overwhelming weight of the cross, Jesus falls a second time. Here is the suffering servant prophesied by Isaiah, who is wounded for our transgressions and crushed for our iniquities. By enduring the pain of the cross, he indeed bears our sins; by his stripes, we are indeed healed.
(Kneel)

All pray: Lord Jesus, you entered into our suffering and thereby sanctified it. Make us not only willing to suffer, but willing to suffer as you did, absorbing violence and hatred through our forgiveness and nonviolence.

(Optional)

Our Father, who art in heaven,
hallowed be thy name;
thy kingdom come,
thy will be done
on earth as it is in heaven.
Give us this day our daily bread,
and forgive us our trespasses,
as we forgive those who trespass against us;
and lead us not into temptation,
but deliver us from evil.
Amen.

Hail Mary, full of grace, the Lord is with thee;
blessed art thou among women,
and blessed is the fruit of thy womb, Jesus.
Holy Mary, Mother of God,
pray for us sinners,
now and at the hour of our death.
Amen.

Glory be to the Father, and to the Son, and to the Holy Spirit; as it was in the beginning, is now, and ever shall be, world without end.
Amen.

(Rise)

All sing:

Pro peccatis suae gentis
Vidit Iesum in tormentis,
Et flagellis subditum.

Bruised, derided, cursed, defiled,
She beheld her tender Child
All with bloody scourges rent.

The Eighth Station

JESUS MEETS THE WOMEN OF JERUSALEM

℣. We adore you, O Christ, and we bless you.
(Genuflect)
℟. Because by your holy cross you have redeemed the world.
(Rise)

Leader: As Jesus is led to Calvary, a great number follow him, including the weeping women of Jerusalem. Jesus turns to them and speaks as judge of the world, saying, "Daughters of Jerusalem, do not weep for me; weep instead for yourselves and for your children."
(Kneel)

All pray: Lord Jesus, you are the Savior who shows us the way out of our sin. But you are also the Judge who shows us we are sinners. Your every move, word, and gesture, especially your violent death, constituted God's judgment on the world. Whenever we are tempted to think that all is well with us, direct our gaze to your cross, where our illusions die.

(Optional)

Our Father, who art in heaven,
hallowed be thy name;
thy kingdom come,
thy will be done
on earth as it is in heaven.
Give us this day our daily bread,
and forgive us our trespasses,
as we forgive those who trespass against us;
and lead us not into temptation,
but deliver us from evil.
Amen.

Hail Mary, full of grace, the Lord is with thee;
blessed art thou among women,
and blessed is the fruit of thy womb, Jesus.
Holy Mary, Mother of God,
pray for us sinners,
now and at the hour of our death.
Amen.

Glory be to the Father, and to the Son, and to the Holy Spirit; as it was in the beginning, is now, and ever shall be, world without end.
Amen.

(Rise)

All sing:

Vidit suum dulcem Natum
Moriendo desolatum,
Dum emisit spiritum.

For the sins of his own nation,
Saw him hang in desolation,
Till his Spirit forth he sent.

The Ninth Station

JESUS FALLS FOR THE THIRD TIME

℣. We adore you, O Christ, and we bless you.
(Genuflect)
℟. Because by your holy cross you have redeemed the world.
(Rise)

Leader: Jesus continues to bear the terrible weight of the cross—a cross so heavy that it causes him to fall for a third time. Bearing the weight of our sin, and entering into our suffering, Jesus now rises to approach the final enemy to be defeated: death itself.
(Kneel)

All pray: Lord Jesus, at the root of sin is fear, especially fear of death. Thus, you journeyed into the realm of death and, by your sacrifice, twisted it back to life. You conquered death precisely by dying. Keep us from living in a world dominated by death and the fear of death, and help us to remember that death does not have the final word.

(Optional)

Our Father, who art in heaven,
hallowed be thy name;
thy kingdom come,
thy will be done
on earth as it is in heaven.
Give us this day our daily bread,
and forgive us our trespasses,
as we forgive those who trespass against us;
and lead us not into temptation,
but deliver us from evil.
Amen.

Hail Mary, full of grace, the Lord is with thee;
blessed art thou among women,
and blessed is the fruit of thy womb, Jesus.
Holy Mary, Mother of God,
pray for us sinners,
now and at the hour of our death.
Amen.

Glory be to the Father, and to the Son, and to the Holy Spirit; as it was in the beginning, is now, and ever shall be, world without end.
Amen.

(Rise)

All sing:

Eia Mater, fons amoris,
Me sentire vim doloris
Fac, ut tecum lugeam.

O thou Mother! fount of love!
Touch my spirit from above,
Make my heart with thine accord.

The Tenth Station

JESUS IS STRIPPED OF HIS GARMENTS

℣. We adore you, O Christ, and we bless you.
(Genuflect)
℟. Because by your holy cross you have redeemed the world.
(Rise)

Leader: The soldiers take Jesus' clothes and divide them into four shares, a share for each soldier, and cast lots for his tunic, fulfilling the words of the Psalm: "They divided my garments among them, and for my vesture they cast lots." Christ is stripped of everything: reputation, comfort, esteem, food, drink—even the pathetic clothes on his back.
(Kneel)

All pray: Lord Jesus, on the way of the cross, you despised the addictions of wealth, pleasure, power, and honor, and you loved the will of your Father. You were stripped naked, utterly detached from worldly goods. You went into the furthest reaches of godforsakenness in order to bring the divine love even to that darkest place. Grant that we may despise what you despised, and love what you loved.

(Optional)

Our Father, who art in heaven,
hallowed be thy name;
thy kingdom come,
thy will be done
on earth as it is in heaven.
Give us this day our daily bread,
and forgive us our trespasses,
as we forgive those who trespass against us;
and lead us not into temptation,
but deliver us from evil.
Amen.

Hail Mary, full of grace, the Lord is with thee;
blessed art thou among women,
and blessed is the fruit of thy womb, Jesus.
Holy Mary, Mother of God,
pray for us sinners,
now and at the hour of our death.
Amen.

Glory be to the Father, and to the Son, and to the Holy Spirit; as it was in the beginning, is now, and ever shall be, world without end.
Amen.

(Rise)

All sing:

Fac, ut ardeat cor meum
In amando Christum Deum
Ut sibi complaceam.

Make me feel as thou hast felt;
Make my soul to glow and melt
With the love of Christ my Lord.

The Eleventh Station

JESUS IS CRUCIFIED

℣. We adore you, O Christ, and we bless you.
(Genuflect)
℟. Because by your holy cross you have redeemed the world.
(Rise)

Leader: Jesus is crucified between two criminals, saying, "Father, forgive them, they know not what they do." Dying on a Roman instrument of torture, undergoing excruciating pain, he allows the full force of the world's hatred and dysfunction to wash over him, to spend itself on him. And he responds not with violence or resentment but with forgiveness.
(Kneel)

All pray: Lord Jesus, in your Crucifixion, you took away the sin of the world, swallowing it up in the divine mercy. Through your perfect sacrifice as high priest, eternal life has been made available to the whole of humanity. Stir up your Church to deepen its participation in this eternal act through the Mass, where we unite our sacrifices with yours.

(Optional)

Our Father, who art in heaven,
hallowed be thy name;
thy kingdom come,
thy will be done
on earth as it is in heaven.
Give us this day our daily bread,
and forgive us our trespasses,
as we forgive those who trespass against us;
and lead us not into temptation,
but deliver us from evil.
Amen.

Hail Mary, full of grace, the Lord is with thee;
blessed art thou among women,
and blessed is the fruit of thy womb, Jesus.
Holy Mary, Mother of God,
pray for us sinners,
now and at the hour of our death.
Amen.

Glory be to the Father, and to the Son, and to the Holy Spirit; as it was in the beginning, is now, and ever shall be, world without end.
Amen.

(Rise)

All sing:

Sancta Mater, istud agas,
Crucifixi fige plagas
Cordi meo valide.

Holy Mother! pierce me through;
In my heart each wound renew
Of my Savior crucified.

The Twelfth Station

JESUS DIES ON THE CROSS

℣. We adore you, O Christ, and we bless you.
(Genuflect)
℟. Because by your holy cross you have redeemed the world.
(Rise)

Leader: From the cross, Jesus says "Consummatum est"—"It is finished." The work of the Lord has been brought to fulfillment. He gives out a loud cry, and breathes his last. Above the crucified God hangs a sign placed by Pontius Pilate and written out in Hebrew, Greek, and Latin: "Jesus the Nazorean, the King of the Jews."
(Kneel)

All pray: Lord Jesus, you are the new David, the one who fulfills salvation history and finally rescues humanity. Help us to announce the message that Pilate first announced unwittingly, the message that every person was born to hear: that you are the new King.

(Optional)

Our Father, who art in heaven,
hallowed be thy name;
thy kingdom come,
thy will be done
on earth as it is in heaven.
Give us this day our daily bread,
and forgive us our trespasses,
as we forgive those who trespass against us;
and lead us not into temptation,
but deliver us from evil.
Amen.

Hail Mary, full of grace, the Lord is with thee;
blessed art thou among women,
and blessed is the fruit of thy womb, Jesus.
Holy Mary, Mother of God,
pray for us sinners,
now and at the hour of our death.
Amen.

Glory be to the Father, and to the Son, and to the Holy Spirit; as it was in the beginning, is now, and ever shall be, world without end.
Amen.

(Rise)

All sing:

Tui Nati vulnerati,
Tam dignati pro me pati,
Poenas mecum divide.

Let me share with thee his pain,
Who for all my sins was slain,
Who for me in torments died.

The Thirteenth Station

JESUS IS TAKEN DOWN FROM THE CROSS AND LAID IN THE ARMS OF MARY

℣. We adore you, O Christ, and we bless you.
(Genuflect)
℟. Because by your holy cross you have redeemed the world.
(Rise)

Leader: After the Crucifixion, Jesus is taken from the cross and laid in the arms of Mary, the definitive Ark of the Covenant, who carried the incarnate Word in her very womb. At his birth, Mary placed Jesus in a manger, where animals eat. Now, at his death, she presents him as food for the life of the world.
(Kneel)

All pray: Lord Jesus, the Blessed Virgin Mary cradled you in her arms. Marked with your blood, she presented your sacrifice to us and for us. In her offering of your body, may we be reminded of the Church's continual offering of your Body in the Eucharist.

(Optional)

Our Father, who art in heaven,
hallowed be thy name;
thy kingdom come,
thy will be done
on earth as it is in heaven.
Give us this day our daily bread,
and forgive us our trespasses,
as we forgive those who trespass against us;
and lead us not into temptation,
but deliver us from evil.
Amen.

Hail Mary, full of grace, the Lord is with thee;
blessed art thou among women,
and blessed is the fruit of thy womb, Jesus.
Holy Mary, Mother of God,
pray for us sinners,
now and at the hour of our death.
Amen.

Glory be to the Father, and to the Son, and to the Holy Spirit; as it was in the beginning, is now, and ever shall be, world without end.
Amen.

(Rise)

All sing:

Fac me tecum pie flere,
Crucifixo condolere,
Donec ego vixero.

Let me mingle tears with thee,
Mourning him who mourned for me,
All the days that I may live.

The Fourteenth Station

JESUS IS LAID IN THE TOMB

℣. We adore you, O Christ, and we bless you.
(Genuflect)
℟. Because by your holy cross you have redeemed the world.
(Rise)

Leader: Joseph of Arimathea, a secret admirer of Jesus, comes courageously to ask for the body of the Lord, and a group of women who had accompanied Jesus from Galilee watch carefully to see where he is buried. His enemies had closed in on him, and most of his intimate friends had fled in fear, but these faithful disciples stay with Jesus until the end.
(Kneel)

All pray: Lord Jesus, make our discipleship as complete and consistent as the women who followed you from Galilee to the grave. You went to the cross because you love your Father's will; let we who love you go to that same bitter end, knowing that the stone of our resting place will, like yours, be one day rolled away. Fill our hearts with the joy of the empty tomb, and make us bold in sharing the Good News of your Resurrection.

(Optional)

Our Father, who art in heaven,
hallowed be thy name;
thy kingdom come,
thy will be done
on earth as it is in heaven.
Give us this day our daily bread,
and forgive us our trespasses,
as we forgive those who trespass against us;
and lead us not into temptation,
but deliver us from evil.
Amen.

Hail Mary, full of grace, the Lord is with thee;
blessed art thou among women,
and blessed is the fruit of thy womb, Jesus.
Holy Mary, Mother of God,
pray for us sinners,
now and at the hour of our death.
Amen.

Glory be to the Father, and to the Son, and to the Holy Spirit; as it was in the beginning, is now, and ever shall be, world without end.
Amen.

(Rise)

All sing:

Iuxta Crucem tecum stare,
Et me tibi sociare
In planctu desidero.

By the cross with thee to stay;
There with thee to weep and pray;
Is all I ask of thee to give.

CLOSING PRAYER

From St. Thérèse of Lisieux's Act of Oblation to Merciful Love

All pray: I thank you, O my God, for all the graces you have granted me, especially the grace of making me pass through the crucible of suffering. It is with joy I shall contemplate you on the Last Day carrying the scepter of your cross. Since you deigned to give me a share in this very precious cross, I hope in heaven to resemble you and to see shining in my glorified body the sacred stigmata of your Passion.
Amen.

In the name of the Father, and of the Son,
and of the Holy Spirit.
Amen.